Art Goddard
The Lion Tamer

TATE PUBLISHING, LLC

Published in the United States of America
by Tate Publishing, LLC
127 East Trade Center Terrace
Mustang, OK 73064
(888) 361–9473

ISBN: 1-5988622-4-3

Mother was in the hallway talking with Mrs.
Kinkaid. They were being disturbed by some unruly
Middle School boys. Mrs. Kinkaid asked Mother if she
knew anything about middle school boys. Mother said no.
Mrs. Kinkaid said, "We need a lion tamer." At that time
Mr. Goddard popped out of his classroom, having heard
enough of their unruly behavior. Quickly, with authority,
he corrected the situation. Mother then turned to Mrs.
Kinkaid: "I think you have found your lion tamer."

-*Susan Santangelo*
former student, collegue and friend

ACKNOWLEDGEMENTS

There are so many people to thank for all their help and input with this book.

Other than naming individuals, I want to thank you. You know who you are–take a bow. To those who proof read from The Kinkaid School, Fair Haven United Methodist Church, The Methodist Men, the "morning gang," where I would have my "second" breakfast every day, and friends who do not fall into any of those groups, thank you.

Finally, to my family, who encouraged me to do this. I still say no one is really going be interested in reading this. My life was ordinary. Thank you, Ruth, for 51 years of marriage, and to my son, who would come to my help. How many times would you hear, "Dave! Help! I hit something. I think I have lost the pages to my book."
Thank you all.

TABLE OF CONTENTS

PREFACE

Looking back over my many years here on earth, I realize how many times my life decisions have changed. I have always had a very strong faith in God, and I believe he has guided me through all these many years.

When I was in the third grade, the teacher asked us to write what we wanted to do in life. I really had no idea. That is an awfully early time in life to have an idea. There was a bell tower near the school that sounded the time every fifteen minutes. While I was waiting for a thought to write about, the clock sounded. We called the clock the "town clock." I wrote a very short statement saying that what I wanted to do was to wind the town clock. The teacher embarrassed me by reading this aloud, and for many years I was teased about this. I never wound the clock.

When I was in junior high, my father encouraged me to play baseball. I dreamed of being a professional baseball player. I never did that.

In high school my mother encouraged me to take piano and voice lessons. I dreamed of being an opera singer. I never did it.

In college I took courses in diplomatic history and

studied several languages. I thought I wanted to be a diplomat and work for the state department. I never did.

In the back of my mind, I had the idea of being a teacher but never gave it much serious thought. In graduate school I prepared to become a teacher. But before I had more than a few months of teaching, I found myself spending over 3 ½ years in the military. I believe that was the last prep for what I would do for life. Even going into the service, the diplomatic profession was what I considered.

After discharge from the army, I went into teaching and found myself at The Kinkaid School in Houston, Texas, where I taught and administered the middle school classes for 42 years. After retirement in 1988, I went back to work evaluating faculty for 8 more years. Even now, 2003, I do not feel I have ever left.

I found in Houston my calling, my family, more friends, and I never looked back.

Art Goddard

CHAPTER 1

BEFORE THE WAR

My lifetime has spanned the greater part of the 20th Century. I believe that an autobiography of this type should include not only one's personal history, but also the family history and its influence on my development. Much of the history of the time will be included in this work.

I was born on June 21, 1918, in Williamstown, Massachusetts. My mother was Mary Catherine Leslie Goddard. She was born on September 20, 1892, in Fitchburg, Massachusetts, and she died on November 23,1991, in Houston, Texas. She had passed her ninety-ninth birthday, and she planned to reach one hundred, but illness took her life.

My mother's parents were Scottish immigrants who entered this country around the year 1890. They took up residence in Fitchburg, Massachusetts. Mother's mother was Mary Henderson Leslie. She was a hard working and very determined lady. Her husband, my grandfather, was William D. Leslie. Both my grandmother and my grandfather came from Dundee, Scotland. I never learned much about him, but I believe he was an alcoholic and a drifter. They had four children, all girls. Mother was the oldest. Grandfather Leslie did not contribute much financially to the family. One of my mother's memories of him involved searching for him at local taverns to tell him to come home for dinner. One day William Leslie left home, and the family never saw him again. Mother always believed that he had returned to Scotland.

To increase family income, my grandmother took in laundry and, after a few years, she took in boarders. My mother, being the oldest child, dropped out of school in order to help my grandmother.

After several years my grandmother divorced William Leslie because of desertion. A few months later she married John Duffus Nicols, one of her boarders. This man was the only grandfather I ever knew.

When Mother dropped out of school, she worked in a shirt making factory. The work was very hard on her. It was a sweat shop. She developed consumption, and doctors advised the family to send her out of the city to live in the countryside. Although the family could not afford this, some neighbors who had immigrated from Holland, Mr. and Mrs. Eugene Moon, came to her aid. Uncle Gene, as Mother called him, was an engineer on the Fitchburg Railroad. Mother spent many hours with them. They had no children, but a niece, Florence Palmer, spent many weeks with them. Florence was my mother's age, and the two became inseparable friends. When Eugene Moon reached retirement age, he bought a small farm in East Meredith, New York. This little village is located in a narrow valley of the foothills of the Catskill Mountains. A railroad, the Ulster and Delaware, paralleled the road on which their farm was located. "Uncle Gene" was very happy there because of the railroad. When they heard about my mother's health problems, they invited her to stay with them until she recovered. Mother not only recovered, but she grew stronger and healthy.

Upon returning to Fitchburg several months later, Mother went to work for the Fitchburg and Leominster Street Railway. This company had developed an amusement park called Whalem Park. This park not only had rides, benches, and a small lake, but also a well known summer theater. Mother worked at the theater and was fascinated by the various shows she saw there. I know that her love of the theater was passed on to me.

Both of my parents were church going. Mother became the alto soloist in the choir of the local Congregational Church. She also acted in plays, was a member of the YWCA, played volleyball, and became a good basketball player. It was during this time that she met my father.

My father's name was Lester Herbert Goddard. He was born November 23, 1887, in Rindge, New Hampshire. His mother was Sarah Elizabeth Barrett, and his father was Elmer Daniel Goddard. My grandfather Goddard had a sister, Thera Goddard, who married one of my grandmother's brothers, Frederick Barrett. Grandmother Goddard's mother was the daughter of Samuel Wilson, who became known as "Uncle Sam" by soldiers and others as he prepared and distributed food supplies at the time of the War of 1812. He signed the food boxes as U.S. Wilson and soon the soldiers called him "Uncle Sam." The supplies were so badly needed, he represented what the country could give. From this, came the nickname for our country, "Uncle Sam." I doubt that he resembled current pictures of "Uncle Sam."

On the Barrett side of the family my ancestry has been traced back to Concord, Massachusetts, where supplies of munitions were hidden from the British on the family farm. When the British marched to Concord at the start of the Revolution, one of their goals was to get the ammunition.

The Goddard side of the family has been traced all the way to Europe long before the American Revolution. William and Elisabeth Miles Goddard were the progenitors of the particular part of the family from which I am descended. William had been a high ranking officer in Cromwell's army at the time of the Puritan Revolution in England.

After Cromwell's defeat, William and his wife Elisabeth Miles, with their three sons, came to the New World and settled near Boston. Soon there were three more sons, and I'm directly descended from the youngest of those last three sons, Edward Goddard. Edward and his father and some of the other sons obtained land grants in the Boston area and in New Hampshire. They enjoyed farming along with a considerable amount of carpentry work.

Tracing down from William and Elisabeth Goddard, some of the descendents attended Harvard and became preachers or teachers. One became a member of the Massachusetts legislature for a few years, and some practiced law. They all remained in New England.

My father and his parents moved from Rindge, New Hampshire to Fitchburg, Massachusetts. After graduating from Fitchburg High School, Father went to work for the Railway Express Company. He met mother at the local Congregational Church, and it wasn't long before they married. About this same time my mother's sister, Ruby Leslie, married Clinton Barrett, who was my father's double first cousin. Clinton also worked for the Railway Express as its agent in Williamstown, Massachusetts. My father became its agent in Ayer, Massachusetts, but when his cousin Clinton was transferred to Athol, Massachusetts, my father replaced him in Williamstown.

During World War I, my father's job was considered essential for the war effort, so he was deferred. His father, my grandfather, became very ill in 1917 and died about a year before I was born. From what I have heard about the cause of his death, I believe it may have been colon cancer. After my grandfather's death, Grandmother Goddard came to live with us a few months after I was born in Williamstown.

Mother and Father lived in a small apartment over the court house in Williamstown. I was born in that apartment on June 21, 1918. After grandmother joined us, the apartment was too small for the family so they moved into a duplex on Water Street next to a "Ma and Pop" grocery store. As a youngster, I was spoiled by the Tashes, who owned the store. Many an ice cream cone, a piece of fruit or whatever I wanted they gave me. The Tash family had come to the United States a few years earlier from Beirut, Lebanon. I came to appreciate how well immigrants could adapt to American ways in a small New England town. They were devoted Roman Catholic and were well received by their church as well as the townspeople in general.

My father had inherited several acres of timber land in New Hampshire. He sold off many of the tall pines for lumber, and with that money he bought a comfortable two story house with more than two acres of garden space on Water Street. We moved into that house in 1923. The house is still there, but it has become a restaurant.

By the time I entered the public schools we had been living in that house for several months. The house had two attics and two cellars. We didn't know about the second cellar for several years until one day our dog was burying a bone in the dirt wall of the cellar, and part of the wall caved it. A small piece of pottery, arrow heads, and other things that we found made us realize that early settlers may have taken refuge there. Father also discovered that the house had been a "way stop" on the "Underground Railroad" used to help runaway slaves escape into Canada. These discoveries increased my interest in history.

My early days in school were not very good, I'm afraid. I was often in trouble. I talked too much, didn't pay attention, and was inclined to bring a pin to school in order to prick the student in front of me. One day, instead of going to school, I hid out in a small forest just off the path I usually followed to the school. My family found me before the day was over, and I know I was punished, but I have forgotten how. I never tried that again, and soon not only my behavior but also my grades improved.

Williamstown is a beautiful place. It lies in a narrow valley in the Berkshire Hills. East of the town is the city of North Adams, Massachusetts, which is only five miles from the town, and east of North Adams is the Mohawk range of mountains. A difficult road called the Mohawk Trail goes over the steep hills off toward Boston, which is approximately 150 miles away along the road known as the Mohawk Trail. West of the town is the range of mountains called the Taconic Mountains. Another difficult road crosses these mountains and extends into New York State toward Albany. Albany is about 45 miles west of Williamstown. North of the town are the Green Moun-

Art Goddard

tains of Vermont, and south of the town is Mt. Greylock, the highest mountain in Massachusetts. The town was called "The Village Beautiful" by Nathanial Hawthorne many years ago.

Williams College is located in the town, and many famous people have homes there. There was always something to do. I enjoyed walking and climbing the hills as did several of my classmates from school. I particularly enjoyed climbing Mt. Greylock, climbing Stone Hill, and walking along the "Long Trail," which is part of the Appalachian Trail that runs just north of the town.

I also loved railroads. My father's job required him to meet all passenger trains entering the town. In those days there were more than a dozen per day. I frequently went with him just to see the trains come in and to collect a timetable from the station master. I developed a large collection of old railroad time tables, but most of them have been lost.

One of my friends was Walter Primmer. His father was an engineer on the Boston and Maine Railroad, which ran through the town. The earliest railroad tunnel in the United States was built under the Hoosac Mountain range just east of Williamstown. The railroad was steam operated, but to reduce gas and smoke during the five mile run through the tunnel, an electric engine was used to pull the train through the tunnel as the steam engines' fires were banked. Walter's father was an engineer on one of these electric engines, and he sometimes took Walter and me along with him for a ride through the tunnel. For me this was great fun.

Nearly every Saturday night I joined friends at the local movie theater where for a dime we could see a double feature. I had no allowance, but I earned some money mowing lawns for neighbors. I had learned how to drive before I was twelve years old, but I didn't get my license until I was sixteen. After receiving my license, I was hired by different neighbors to drive for them. I usually received fifty cents each time I drove one.

While I was in high school, I suffered from a severe hernia. During the depression years my family could not afford to pay for an operation, but the pain became so severe that I had the operation anyway. There were some complications with the surgery, which required me to spend more than two weeks in the hospital and a month in bed at home. That is how I spent that summer vacation just before my freshman year in high school. My doctor wouldn't allow me to take gym or any sports during my freshman, sophomore, and junior years in high school, but I was allowed to walk and go on brief hikes. It was a great disappointment to me and my father. Both of us wanted me to become a baseball player.

During the decade of the 1920s, Father had prospered well. The house he bought on Water Street had two and a half acres of land. Father always loved farming, and he grew great vegetables. His philosophy about gardening was quite simple; prepare the ground, plant the seeds or plants, and let nature do the rest. Weeds never bothered him. His tomatoes, corn, beans, and squash were the envy of his neighbors. Food was in abundance for us.

Mother was not a gardener. Her interests were primarily social. She was an active member of the Williamstown Grange and very active in the Eastern Star. Father was a Mason too. Both of my parents were out frequently in the evenings, and I was with Grandmother Goddard. Grandmother taught me much about the Bible. She read each evening from it until I fell asleep. My mother said later that she had read the entire Bible to me more than twice.

I was very close to Grandmother Goddard, and I had a very sad experience with her in 1933. Mother had taken a part time job in the nearby city of North Adams, and she often didn't return from work until late in the afternoon. Grandmother usually prepared the meals. On a very snowy and cold and windy day in March, I returned home from school. While Grandmother was preparing supper, I practiced on the piano. Brownie, our dog, was barking to come into the house. There was more than a foot of snow on the ground, and Brownie did not enjoy snow. Grandmother had started a small gas heater in the kitchen because it was so cold. She opened the door to let the dog in, and a gust of wind blew flames from the heater onto her. Her dress and apron caught fire. She screamed for help, and when I reached the kitchen she was ablaze. I remembered not to throw water on her, but to smother out the fire. I wrapped her in a throw rug, which did put the fire out, but she was badly burned. Later infection set in on her wounds. Mother would change her dressings many times a day. Mother took up smoking to mask the oder of the infection on Grandmother's wounds. Grandmother died about a month after the fire.

In the 1930s my father had severe financial problems. The Railway Express Company changed his job from a company paying one to a commission job. For a short period of time this was not bad, but as The Depression continued, business, in spite of the presence of the college, dropped off badly. Neither Mother nor I knew that Father had used up all our financial savings, mortgaged the house, and filed for bankruptcy. I was a senior in high school when the story appeared in the local North Adams Transcript newspaper. Not only was the mortgage on the house being foreclosed, but two of our three cars had been sold. The bank allowed him to keep one car and to continue to live in the house, but he had to pay rent.

Mother had stopped working in order to help care for her mother, who was very ill with heart trouble. She tried in vain to find another job. I was about to start college. Thanks to a scholarship, living at home, and a little money I had saved from mowing lawns and working for a short time in a laundry, I was able to pay the necessary fees for starting at Williams College.

My father used the one car we still had to start a taxi business. I drove some for him, but I was a poor taxi driver. It wasn't unusual for me to drive a mile or more beyond the place where I was to pick up a customer. My mind was on my studies.

During summer vacations, my mother and I usually spent a couple weeks with her mother in Fitchburg and a couple of weeks in East Merideth, New York, with the Moons. Mother's mother often rented a cottage on the sea coast for a couple of weeks each summer in spite of the hard times caused by The Depression. My cousin Clint Barrett and I, along with my Aunt Bea (mother's youngest sister), accompanied her. When my cousin Clint was six years old, his mother died of a heart condition, and he had lived with our grandmother since then. Clint's father just couldn't accept the responsibility of caring for his son.

When college started, I signed up for a very heavy course load. It was probably too heavy for someone who had never had to take a final exam when he was in high school. In college, I discovered that my grades would be determined by my final exams. I did not know how to study for such an exam. I did pass all my freshmen courses, but it was difficult for me.

English had been one of my strongest classes while

I was in high school. At Williams my English instructor was the head of the English department. I did very well at first, but around Thanksgiving time the college replaced my professor with a much younger one. I was never able to satisfy him with my writing or interpretation of the literature. During the Christmas vacation I was asked to report to the dean. There were a few others from my English class there also. The dean asked us to request an incomplete grade and to drop the English course. The dean told me that I could substitute an advanced course in French for the English as I was doing so well in French.

As a result, I believe that I am among very few graduates of an "Ivy League" school who had no credit in English. I made up for this after World War II when for three summers I took English courses at Boston University. I did very well there.

I had two very close friends among my classmates at Williams. They were George Dutton and George Cragin. George Dutton lived in Williamstown, but he lived in a dorm at the college. His roommate was George Cragin, who was from Hartford, Connecticut. George Cragin's father was an executive with Aetna Life Insurance Company. I was frequently studying with them in their room. The three of us loved railroads, and we often drove to Albany, New York just to watch the "fleet" (fast trains from New York to Chicago on the New York Central Railroad) go by.

One week George Cragin asked George Dutton and me to go with him to visit his aunt in Boston. She had tickets to two Gilbert and Sullivan operas. George Cragin loved those operas, and he wanted us to become familiar with them also. It was a very enjoyable weekend, and I did fall in love with Gilbert and Sullivan music. That interest is still with me today.

Since I had no money, I did not join a fraternity, but there was a special club, the Garfield Club, available for those of us who did not join a fraternity. Attending this club gave me some of the fellowship that colleges provide.

I had decided to major in history, but I also took qualifying courses in French German, and Italian. My official minor, however, was political science. I had no idea how important those languages were to be for me later on. My mother had insisted that I sing in our church choir. I sang there while I was in high school and for some years afterward.

I heard that singers in the chapel choir at Williams were paid $25.00 per semester. I tried out for that choir and made it. The wife of the chapel choir director was the organist and choir director of the Williamstown Congregational Church. She hired me as tenor soloist for a dollar and a half per Sunday. Chapel hours and the Congregational Church hours did not conflict, so I was able to sing in both choirs.

I graduated from Williams in 1940, and immediately enrolled in the graduate program for teachers in the North Adams branch of Massachusetts State College. I doubled up on my courses there and received my Master Degree in Education in August 1941.

While I was at Williams I also joined a singing group called "The Bach Choir." The director of this choir was the same who directed the chapel choir. The Bach Choir was invited with a choir from the southern part of Berkshire County to sing with the Boston Symphony Orchestra at their summer retreat at Tanglewood. I sang there under the direction of Sergei Koussevitsky during the summers of 1940 and 1941. I even did some solo work there. The Tanglewood chorus introduced the Randolph Thompson "Alleluia." I was privileged to take part in its first presentation. We sang it acapella for Koussevitsky at a special ceremony given in his honor.

During my college years, the world was becoming increasingly alarmed by the continuing aggression of some European countries such as Germany and Italy. My political science professor in 1940 warned his class that the greatest danger was not in Europe, but in the Pacific against Japan. He predicted that Japan would attack us within the next few months. He was correct.

When German troops invaded Poland in September of 1939, World War II started as England and France announced they were going to the aid of Poland. At this time I was with George Cragin at Dartmouth in New Hampshire, where he was getting his eyes fitted with contact lenses.

We had to spend a couple days awaiting the lenses, so we took advantage of the time and climbed Mt. Washington, the second time I had climbed it. It was so cold and windy that we descended by the cog railroad instead of hiking down.

After George received his contacts, we drove back to Williamstown as classes were about to start. George had a new car equipped with a radio. We turned the radio on and were shocked to hear a broadcast from Warsaw, Poland, saying that "as far as one can see, German planes are coming at us." Suddenly, the radio went silent. Later an announcement was made that England and France announced that a state of war existed with Germany. This marked the start of World War II on September 3, 1939.

While I was working for my Master's Degree in education from the Massachusetts State College at North Adams, the Draft Act was passed. Like all other males over 18 years of age, I had enrolled for possible military service. Under the terms of the act, names were assigned numbers all over the country. First numbers, hence names too, were drawn from a huge glass bowl in Washington. It was like a lottery, and the following day the local newspaper announced that my name had been drawn. I won that lottery! I had to take a physical exam, but because of an irregular heart beat, I did not pass it. I was classified as 1B, which meant I would be re-examined later. In late November 1941, I was called for another physical, but I failed to pass it again.

After the Japanese attack on Pearl Harbor on December 7, 1941, I tried to enlist in the navy, but again I did not pass the physical.

I received my Master of Education degree in late August 1941 and accepted a teaching position at the Bridgeton Academy in North Bridgeton, Maine. I started work there right after the Christmas vacation.

Although I had been a history major, the position at Bridgeton was to teach upper classes in French and English. In addition, I was assigned to teach a course in general science at the freshman level. I was assigned other duties too, such as assistant dorm master of the older boys' dorm, to be the school librarian, and was in charge of certain school publications. I was expected to help with the winter sports too. I enjoyed the teaching there very much even though I was younger than many of my students. At that time one had to have had at least two years of college in order to become a pilot in the army air force, hence several of the boys were in their early twenties. I learned a lot about students and teaching! It was awkward for me to see that men older than me were in their rooms at curfew.

The shadow of the war was always with us during

those days. Although I had a 1B deferment, I was called for another physical in January and again in March 1942. Both times I was turned down because of my heart problem. In April 1942, I received a notice to report on April 24, 1942, in Portland, Maine, for another check up. This time I passed the physical and found myself a member of the U. S. Army before the end of the day.

I had enjoyed very much the teaching I had done at the Bridgeton Academy. I learned a great deal about schools during the short time I was there, and I felt that I would continue in education after the war. I had been very uneasy about being rejected for service. I had felt that it was my duty to serve, and now I had my chance.

CHAPTER 2

DRAFTED

It was a rainy afternoon when I reached Portland, Maine. The next morning I was expected to have a lengthy physical at the Selective Service Office. I was so certain that I would be rejected again that I left my clothes and possessions at the school. I had been assured by the head master that I would not be taken even if I passed the physical because I was essential to the school, and he was head of the draft board in Portland at the time. Unfortunately for me he was hospitalized and unable to supervise the draft board when they reviewed my records. I did pass the physical and I was sworn in to the Army before noon on that day. I was pleased that I had finally made it, but I was scared about the future. We were given one hour to make necessary arrangements as we were to leave by a train that afternoon for Ft. Devens in Massachusetts. News of my being drafted shocked the folks at Bridgeton as well as my parents. The school agreed to pack my things and send them to my parent's home in Williamstown.

The train ride from Portland to Ft. Devens in Ayre, Massachusetts, took me through familiar territory, but seemed unusual long on that Friday April 24, 1942. Accompanied by other draftees whom I did not know, we speculated about our future. I felt comfortable with a couple of the draftees, and we planned to try to stay together.

At Fort Devens we exchanged civilian clothes for military, which we would be wearing for years to come. Lining up in one of the buildings, we awaited our turn for inoculations. I dreaded the needle because some men in front of me had fainted when they received the shots. A very strong, boisterous soldier of Polish ancestry directly in front of me had been bragging about what he would do to the Japanese. As the medic approached him with a needle in his hand, he looked at the needle and collapsed. Surprisingly the shots did not bother me at all.

That evening my Aunt Bea, my mother's youngest sister, my grandmother, and my mother who was in Fitchburg visiting her family, drove over to the fort to visit me. They were not allowed to enter, nor was I allowed to leave the building to be with them, but we were allowed to visit for a half hour through the wired fence surrounding the area.

Later that night, we received a typical experience of army life. About two o'clock in the morning, an air raid alarm sounded. We were forced to double time to an area about a mile away. Almost as soon as we reached the destination, an all clear sounded and we were ordered to double time back. This was only a drill, but I discovered that I was very weak and had a long way to go in build up strength enough to keep up with the others. I decided to try as hard as I could!

The next day we were ordered to take our official papers and a barracks bag full of our army clothes to the parade grounds. We lined up single file for instructions and a roll call. We marched to the railroad yard at Ft. Devens, where we found four troop trains steaming and ready to go. We were ordered again to line up single file. Because we knew each other, I stood between two soldiers who had been friendly, and we wanted to stay together. Orders came for us to count off by fours. All number ones boarded the first train, number twos the second, and so on. I boarded train number three and found it was going to Fort Bragg in North Carolina. I never saw my two buddies again. Fort Bragg was a training camp for paratroopers and for field artillery. I prayed that I would be in field artillery as I had never flown, and I was terrified of heights in spite of my earlier hikes in the mountains. It turned out that I was assigned to field artillery.

I was assigned to a gun crew and trained on 105mm Howitzers. We had regular basic including infantry training, long marches, etc. We spent several hours each day with the cannon too. It did not take me long to become familiar with that cannon, and I did well on various tests involving it.

Ft. Bragg was one of the hottest camps in the country, both for military activities and also temperature. Basic training was usually for sixteen weeks. During the first two weeks we were quarantined. While at Ft. Bragg, I received a few weekend passes, but I never had enough money to go far. One weekend I went by bus to Winston-Salem, North Carolina. I was the only person in uniform in the hotel lobby where I had obtained a room for the night. None of my buddies were with me. I enjoyed a great meal in the hotel restaurant and was told it would be charged to my room. The next morning I ate there again. As I went to pay my bill for the room and meals, the clerk told it was all paid for by one of the customers in the hotel. I considered this to be an example of the graciousness most people showed toward service men. This made me feel good, but I regretted that I never found out who the benefactor was.

Another memory of those days is not as pleasant. My mother and my Aunt Bea came to Fayetteville to visit me. I joined them in a walk in downtown Fayetteville. We discovered how unfair life could be for Blacks. As we were walking along the streets of Fayetteville, we noticed a group of Blacks walking toward us. In front of us walking toward the Blacks were several citizens of the city. As the Blacks got closer, some of them crossed to the other side of the street, but one elderly lady was very slow in moving.

A couple of the children among the civilians ran up to her, and I thought they were going to help her, but instead they shoved her into the gutter, yelling at her to get out of the way. Although there were policemen nearby, none went to her aid. The other Blacks seemed to ignore it too. I didn't know what to do. A couple soldiers walking behind me told me to forget it.

That weekend in Fayetteville was the last time I saw anyone from my family except in New York on the day before I sailed for Europe. Some of my buddies received furloughs to go home, but I didn't. One day in June 1942 we were called into a special formation. The battalion commander called out several of us by name, including me. We were told that we would be sent the next day to officer candidate school since we had the correct qualifications for it. That evening our sadistic drill sergeant placed all of us whose names had been called

Art Goddard

on latrine duty. He forced us to clean everything on our hands and knees throughout the night. We had no rest.

At reveille the next morning our battery captain announced that the entire battalion was alerted for overseas service and that all special orders had been canceled. We were now in the 431st Automatic Anti-aircraft Weapons Battalion. This new assignment was to be our permanent one. We joined a small group and boarded a train for Camp Stewart near Savannah, Georgia. I was assigned to Battery D of that battalion and remained with it throughout the war. Since we were a separate battalion, we could be attached to any other military unit if needed. We were now trained on 40mm Bofor anti-aircraft guns and fifty caliber machine guns as infantry.

Training at Camp Stewart was mostly for the infantry. There was only one 40mm cannon that we could use. Only a small group could work at one time. We had a sleeve target drawn by a plane slowly over us that we could fire at.

Most of us simply watched a few others shoot at targets. They almost always missed it too. I thought that this wasn't much preparation for what might be coming. We had so much to learn!

At Camp Stewart we survived a hurricane by standing almost waist deep in water, holding our tents down. Right after the storm I received a bite from a black widow spider on my right elbow. A battery medic lanced my swollen elbow and placed my arm in a sling. I was excused from most duties and did not have to salute officers for the next two weeks. I enjoyed the rest.

While we were at Camp Stewart, I was able to spend a weekend in the city of Savannah. It was a great place for me, a historian, to have free time. The weekend passed much too quickly, but I took advantage of the time to write a considerable number of letters, as well as do some sightseeing and eat fresh fruit, especially Georgia peaches. Shortly after returning from the weekend in Savannah, we received orders to go to Fort Dix, New Jersey. This was a jumping off place for loading transports for overseas. We knew our time had come. When we arrived at Ft. Dix, I called my parents and arranged to meet them the next day in New York City. We spent the day together as they came in on a day excursion from North Adams. I remember how my parents became emotional when we took the Staten Island Ferry ride and passed the "QUEEN MARY," which was loaded with troops and leaving the port.

I knew that I would be doing the same thing, not on the "QUEEN MARY," but on some other troop transport very soon. The "QUEEN MARY" was by far the fastest troop transport and was able to travel without navy escort and outrun Axis ships easily.

On the day after my visit with my parents, we returned to New York City by trucks and boarded the troop transport "ORCADES," which had been a luxury liner on the Australian run of the Canard Steamship Company. This ship was operated by the British Navy, and my sleeping quarters were on the lowest deck. I was assigned a hammock there, but I spend most of the time on deck while we were at sea.

During the ten days it took to cross the Atlantic, I had plenty of time to reflect on all that had happened since April 24, 1942. I had survived basic training, which had been shortened to six weeks. I had had several weekend passes, but I never had a furlough, and I had lost an opportunity to become an officer. Now I wondered what my chances for survival were. I did not feel like military material, but I wanted to do my duty, and I prayed that I could and would survive.

When I was drafted, I weighed a mere 122 lbs. At Ft. Dix I weighed 132 lbs. Military life was making me stronger. My shoulders were so narrow that it was difficult for me to balance a rifle on them. Often my rifle fell off during drills and marching. I was not strong; it was all I could do to lift my barracks bag. On the rifle range I thought I was doing well, but I never hit my target. However, upon examination of the targets, one target next to mine had received several accurate shots. That target had not been assigned to anyone, and it was determined that I had shot at the wrong target. I was terrified of heights, and much of the obstacle course had been a nightmare, but I kept trying.

Rather than brood over these things, I decided to make friends with members of my battery. The 431st AAA–AW Battalion had four combat batteries and one headquarters battery.

The batteries were named A,B,C,D, and Headquarters. I was assigned to Battery D, which consisted of 176 soldiers, twenty four vehicles trucks and jeeps, eight 40 mm anti- aircraft cannon, and four 50 cal. machine guns. I was placed on gun crew number eight of the second platoon. I was classified as a gunner.

Looking back on this, I am amazed that out of the 176 men, 129 of us stayed together throughout the war. Of those who were not with us at the end, a few had died in action, a few were seriously wounded, a few transferred to other military units, and a few were given early discharge for some reason or another and sent home.

Upon boarding the "ORCADES," we were informed that our destination was England. The long voyage across the Atlantic Ocean gave us good opportunities to become better acquainted with each other.

Most of the men in my battery were from Pennsylvania and were of Italian or Polish ancestry. There were a few from New York, a couple from New England (including me), and a few from the South. The first lieutenant in charge of the second platoon was from Georgia. I came to know him very well. We had mutual interests in history. Even though he was an officer and I an enlisted man, we became good friends.

On board the ship I became acquainted with a very unusual soldier from Pennsylvania. He was eccentric and claimed to be an undercover officer spying on our staff officers. He insisted that he was to watch certain officers for un-American activities. In reality he was only a private who wanted to get out of the army.

One time, as we were preparing to leave the British Isles, he went absent without leave. When he finally returned, he insisted that he had been looking for some of our men who had overstayed a pass in Glasgow. He himself was ten days overdue.

He was court-marshalled, given a section eight, and sent back to the United States where he was discharged. Some time later I received a letter from him stating that he had a good job, was making good money, had known how to get out of the army, and had succeeded.

Since the army often grouped us alphabetically, it was natural that many of my buddies had last names beginning with a G. One was the driver of the captain's jeep. He and I went through several experiences together that I will relate later. Another buddy was from Massachusetts. He had a very traumatic experience when he accidentally hit the butterfly trigger of a 50 cal. machine gun which he was cleaning. The bullet killed another one of our buddies. This soldier never recovered from that experience, and he had considerable psychiatric help.

Art Goddard

One of the Italian-American buddies from Homer City, Pennsylvania, became my best friend. His name was Marino Gazza, but we called him "Goggs." He had been a truck driver before the war, and during basic training he was assigned to teach others how to drive a two and a half ton truck. He had great patience with me. It took all my strength just to turn the wheel of such a truck. I was very nervous and unsure about driving, but he kept me going. I passed the course and received an army driving license, thanks to "Goggs."

The trip across the Atlantic was very long, rough, and dangerous. We left New York City and were hardly out of sight of land when we were informed that we would first go to Halifax, Nova Scotia, and await more escort ships. The British crew on our transport informed us that there were "Wolf Packs" of German submarines waiting to attack our convoy.

When we left Halifax, there were so many ships in our convoy that we could not see beyond them. Our ship was near the middle of the convoy. The British crew demonstrated proper ways to abandon ship, including climbing down a single strand of rope. There were not enough life boats for all on board, but each had his own life preserver.

As the convoy continued to the northeast, we followed a " zig–zag" pattern in order to make it difficult for submarines to fire their torpedoes. This procedure slowed the convoy down. No convoy could go faster than its slowest ship, and there were several slow moving merchant ships heavily laden with supplies along with us. We were very vulnerable to attack. Several days out of Halifax in the North Atlantic, a wolf pack of submarines closed in on us. Our destroyers and cruisers began to dart in and out among the ships. I was terrified and expected that at any moment a torpedo would strike us. The escorting navy ships set off smoke screens in order to hide the troop transports and merchant ships. Destroyers dropped depth charges around us. Through gaps in the smoke screen, I saw heavy black smoke and fire from one of the ships in the distance. One of our merchant ships had been hit, and before our trip was over more than a dozen ships went down.

Several of my buddies and I were hugging the rails on deck when suddenly a submarine emerged through the sea near us. The submarine nosed up and settled back into the water. We saw no signs of a crew emerging from the sinking sub.

Later on that same day the sea became very rough as a gale struck us. The ship's crew was happy about the rough water, but most of us were seasick. I was one of the few who did not suffer from sea sickness, perhaps because I had eaten many dry crackers. I had heard that the crackers would help ward off sea sickness, and they did in my case.

Some of my buddies were dangerously ill. One buddy from Pittsburgh, Pennsylvania, had been ill from the time he first stepped on the gangplank leading from the pier to the ship. His sickness lasted the entire trip, but later, on dry land, he served as an excellent cook. He survived the war, but was very ill again on the voyage back to the States.

As we sailed on through the storm and then into the darkness of night, the ocean quieted considerably. In the late afternoon, dolphins, whales, and schools of smaller fish were swimming close to the shop, and sea gulls were flying around the ships. We were approaching the island of Iceland. We entered the harbor of Reykjavik where a few of our ships left the convoy. The rest of us sailed on. As daylight faded into darkness, the speed of the convoy picked up. A thick fog closed in on us. The British crew was happy about that. The closer we got to the British Isles, the more dangerous the trip would be. It was foggy most of the next day. As night arrived, the fog lifted. We kept on through the night as fast as the convoy could go. I had spent the last two days awaiting a possible submarine or air attack.

Like others on the deck we were searching the sky for planes. Suddenly general quarters were sounded. Was this going to be an attack? Several planes were spotted closing in on us, but the British crew shouted with joy. They were British fighter planes come out to escort us into port.

We reached the port of Belfast in Northern Ireland where some more of our ships left the convoy. The rest sailed on through the Irish Sea to the English port of Liverpool. We had to wait offshore for several hours. Liverpool had just been bombed and the port area was ablaze with fires. Some ships in the port were burning also. At about 2:00 A.M. we were able to approach a pier and unload.

As we marched through the streets of Liverpool, we could see soldiers, police, and others trying to put out fires and clear debris from the burning buildings. The horrible smell of burning human flesh was everywhere. We continued to march to the railroad yard where we boarded a troop train that took us to Tidworth Barracks on Salisbury Plain in southern England. As the dawn came up while the train was passing through the country side, I was impressed by the beautiful gardens so many houses had.

That night the Axis propagandist, Lord Haw Haw, in his radio broadcast welcomed us by naming our military units. He identified some of our officers by their personal names. He promised that German troops would soon eliminate us. WE HAD ARRIVED!

CHAPTER 3

TORCH

Tidworth was already protected by British anti-aircraft positions. We were ordered to relieve the British. As a result, we were to be among the first Americans other than some army air force units to be on active duty in the European Theater of Operations.

Much infantry training, guard duty, and a good three day pass to London marked our stay at Tidworth. I remember well my first purchase at a British canteen. I did not understand the British coin system, so I just gave the clerk a handful of mixed American and British money. She took most of it. Later I found that I had been taken for as much as five dollars. This experience made me learn about British money.

One of our lieutenants, who was well liked by the men, was instructed to take us on a twenty-five mile hike in one day. We marched all the way to Stonehenge, as he believed everyone should have a chance to visit Stonehenge. We were exhausted when we arrived there, and I thought I could see smoke coming out of my shoes. My feet were so hot and sore. We knew we would rest for a few minutes there and then walk all the way back to Tidworth Barracks. Most of us felt that we just couldn't do it. At his own expense, however, our lieutenant had arranged for chartered buses to meet us and take us back to camp. What a pleasant surprise it was to see those double-decker buses of the Wilts and Dorset Bus Company pull up beside us and realize that we would not have to walk back to camp.

I had a three day pass to visit London. I took a local bus to Salisbury where I crowded into an already overflowing train to go to London. I stood all the way and frequently had to pull my toes out from under some boots.

In Salisbury I noticed many stores had the name "Goddard" on their entrance. I wondered then if my ancestors might have come from there. Genealogy studies in recent days showed that my guess was correct.

Arriving at Victoria Station in London, I took the subway to Kensington where American soldiers were assigned rooms in the Hans Crescent Hotel. The hotel was run by the Red Cross, and we had army cots for sleeping, but we had to go elsewhere for food. Although food in England was rationed and restaurants were limited to charging only five shillings, about a dollar, we did find places to eat. Most meals consisted of fish and chips. That was a good change from army rations.

One night several of my buddies and I located a French restaurant in the subway station at Piccadilly. We had the usual fish and chips along with tea, but to our surprise a waiter left a basket full of French pastries on our table. Eagerly we devoured these pastries and wondered why the waiter and near by patrons were glaring at us.

As we left the restaurant, some American officers who were seated near the door called us over to them. They informed us that those pastries were meant for the entire restaurant and we were expected to take only one each. Boy, were we embarrassed! Not only did I never go by that restaurant again, but I stayed away from the subway station too. I found time to attend the stage show "Rose Marie." Although I had seen the show in New York and also the movie, I enjoyed seeing it again.

During my school days I had often dreamed of visiting London and taking a boat trip on the Thames. Most public buildings were closed, and there was a black out at night, but I did take a short boat ride in the afternoon. My visit to London was enjoyable, but I had to return to camp.

One day, we were told to prepare to leave by train for more training, probably in Scotland. We were given a new APO number–army postal number. It was APO Number One. Immediately some of my buddies said this meant "first to be killed." But it really designated that we were assigned to the First Infantry Division, the "Big Red One." We traveled to Scotland where we spent several days in a castle at Berwick. From there we went to Roseneath by train, and after a few days of training there we went into Glasgow, where we were briefly based in the Pollockshores Estate.

At Berwick and Roseneath, we had had artillery training and even a dry run to get off a ship by climbing over its sides and descending on ropes or a net into barges below. This was done at Loch Lynhe. In Glasgow our training was limited to infantry drills and classroom instruction. It was much too muddy to do much training, so we were allowed to leave camp each afternoon about 4:00 P.M. and take a tram into the heart of the city, and go to a restaurant and even a movie. I took advantage of these passes. I went into town then to the Paramount Theater, and after the show I ate at the Paramount café. The movies usually showed American newsreels, and this made us homesick. Just across the street from the theater was an F. W. Woolworth sign. One of my buddies said it just wasn't real. We had never left the States. Of course, this wasn't true, but we all felt great emotion. Glasgow was far enough away from German airfields, so instead of a black out, they had a brown out. Because of the heavy mud on the estate, we had to carry our socks and boots to the gate. At the gate the army provided buckets of water and towels to wash and dry our feet. We were in dress uniforms, which we had to protect from frequent rain.

After two weeks in Glasgow we went to the port of Grenock where we boarded a troop transport named the " REINA DEL PACIFICO." It had been in Australian service as had the "ORCADES."

Shortly before we boarded the transport in Glasgow, I had a three day weekend pass. I decided to go to Edinburgh to find some of my grandmother's family. My grandmother had several brothers and sisters, but I only knew the name of one of her sisters who lived in Montrose, Scotland, and one brother who lived in Edinburgh. Some of my friends went with me. I looked in the city directory to find my great uncle's name, James Henderson. There were so many pages of people by that name that I gave up. My buddies and I went to church services at St. Giles Cathedral on our last day in Edinburgh. We sat behind a very friendly Scotch family who invited us to have "a wee bit of Scotch lunch" with them. I didn't have time to go. Many years later there was a Scotch lady I hired as an English instructor at the Kinkaid School in Houston. She spoke of inviting some

American soldiers, who sat in front of her at St. Giles, to her home for lunch, but they didn't have time. She mentioned that she thought at first they were from South Africa. I remembered how the Scotch family we met at St. Giles had mistaken us for South Africans at first. We knew then that we had met before.

As we boarded the transport, I helped transfer the luggage from trucks to the cargo hold. Many Scottish citizens were watching us and occasionally one would talk to us. One man came up to me and handed me a bottle of milk. Since milk was rationed, I knew he was taking a great risk. He told me that he knew we were heading for North Africa and not the island of Malta about which rumors were circulating. I had no clue how he knew, but he was correct.

As we left the port of Grenock, one of my buddies and I were standing on the deck speculating about the future. I commented that we would never forget the date we left for combat. It was Columbus Day, October 12, 1942. For several years after the war, he called me on Columbus Day reminding me where we had been and to find out how I was doing. He had become a good friend. He died a few years ago after he passed the age of ninety.

On board ship during the next few weeks, I was assigned to special watch duty with the British crew. My post was on the bridge, and my shift was midnight until 4:00 A.M. and also from noon to 4:00 P.M. This was a good duty because I was excused from everything else. Our ship was the flagship on the convoy heading into the central front of the planned invasion of French North Africa. General Terry Allen, commander of the First Infantry Division, and General Theodore Roosevelt III were on our ship. I sometimes saw them working out on deck while I was on afternoon watch. On the bridge it was often an exciting place to be. During the night shift the British shared tea and biscuits with us. Three members of my battery shared this duty.

My sleeping quarters were on the lowest deck. My hammock was right over one of the tables where we ate. We shared this area with a company of British Commandos with whom we were to land when the time came. The convoy was indeed very large. It stretched out in all directions as far as one could see. Security was very tight. We were not informed officially about our destination until shortly before we landed. We learned later that some maps and other materials had been planted on a carrier that was set adrift and washed ashore in Spain.

These plans indicated that an Allied invasion was to occur in the Balkans, and they were deliberately planted to deceive the Axis agents who might discover the approaching convoy. I have had contradictory information about this, but at the time this was what we understood. After all, Spain was under the dictatorship of Franco, who was friendly with both Italy and Germany. If Franco decided to enter the war on the side of the Axis, we would be cut off at Gibraltar and trapped in the Mediterranean Sea.

Our food on the ship was almost impossible to eat. We were given two meals daily, breakfast and dinner. Both meals consisted of the same things–boiled, soggy potatoes, dried and smelly fish, and tea. After a few days of this, some of the men in my battery joined the British Commandos in revolt. Our first sergeant led the revolt.

The British officer in charge of food was unable to satisfy the men. The British called for help from American officers, including General Terry Allen. The General smelled the food, tasted it, and turned to the British officer asking, "Have you eaten any of this swill?" Boy did we like General Allen for that. Needless to say, our food not only improved, but was actually good after that. General Allen ordered an American staff officer to eat each meal with us and to report to him on its quality.

One night while I was on watch duty, we saw the lights of an ocean liner appearing in the distance and headed directly into the convoy. That ship was lighted, so we knew it belonged to a neutral country, probably Spain or Portugal. Our convoy commander ordered all shops to turn on lights, which would frame the ships, so that the approaching ship would not get among us. What a spectacular sight it was to see the outlines of hundreds of ships as far as one could see light up. The ship turned away from us. Our lights went off, but we knew that the Axis powers knew where we were.

Early Friday morning, November 6, 1942, we passed through the Strait of Gibraltar. Even though it was a moonless night, I could see the outline of the Rock of Gibraltar and the lights of surrounding Spanish villages and towns. All day Friday and Saturday we sailed though the Mediterranean Sea. Hoping to confuse the enemy of our landing plans, we sailed beyond the designated areas. Part of our convoy continued on to the city of Algiers, and the rest of us closed in on the port of Oran, Algeria. Our destination was the resort seaport of Arzeu, a short distance east of Oran. There was a French seaplane base at Arzeu that we were expected to capture. The approach to the harbor was protected by two jetties coming out from the shore. We were expected to sneak under the cover of darkness between these jetties and capture the sea plane base. U.S.troops took the lead rather than the British in approaching the shore. The French in North Africa remembered too well that the British shelled Oran earlier in the war, and many civilians lost their lives at that time. British forces were not popular with the citizens of French North Africa, but American forces were.

How quiet it was in the darkness of that cool November night! The hum of the ship's engines could no longer be heard. The sound of the gentle splash made by the waters of the Mediterranean Sea as the ship glided slowly to its destination was all one could hear. The ship had stopped, and we realized that the expected moment had come.

Sitting on the deck with other members of my battery, I became aware of a soft movement like the shuffling of feet across the decks. Soon the noise of the "Higgins boats," landing craft, was heard as they were lowered into the sea. A muffled shout and the vanishing sound of outboard motors toward the distant Algerian shore were heard, and again all was quiet.

I could see the profiles of the men beside me. How tense they were! Some were thinking of homes and families; some were concerned about their behavior in the events to come; some remembered the last pass we enjoyed in Glasgow. We all knew that our time had come.

My thoughts were dominated by one ridiculous fear that seemed to control my mind. How were we to get from our deck, which was the highest of all decks, into the barge waiting for us nearly sixty feet down? We were to climb down a scramble net into that barge. This terrified me. It wasn't going to be easy with a sixty pound field pack on my back, a bayonet dangling from the hip, my rifle slung over my shoulder, and my helmet loose and balanced on my head.

As I started down my bayonet tangled with the scramble net. The space for my hands to grip the rope wasn't more than an inch, and I kept trying to step on the soldier below me just as the one above stepped on my knuckles. Scramble nets were made entirely of rope, and they gave way to pressure. Because several soldiers used them at the same time, they swayed constantly and seemed to try to shake the occupants into the sea.

With an effort to control my fears, I started down. At first the net was taut against the side of the ship, and I thought I could manage that, but when I passed the bulge of the ship, the ladder swayed and shook. My hold on the ropes tightened. Thinking that I must be almost down, I made the mistake of looking down. There was nothing to be seen through the darkness. A sickening wave of nausea swept over me as I thought, "What if the barge has already gone?" There was nothing else to do but to continue climbing down.

My left foot searched for the next strand of rope, and the shifting of my weight caused the rope to break. A fraction of a second later I was picking myself up from the bottom of the barge. I recognized the voice of my first sergeant saying, "Well, that's one way to do it. Are your all right?" I was all in one piece. I crawled to my assigned position in the barge and relaxed in waist deep water.

What a relief it was to get off the ship! I had fallen about sixteen feet and landed on top of the first sergeant, who had tried to catch me and had broken my fall. I became aware of the situation around us. There were sounds of heavy gun fire close by, and machine guns were firing at us. Tracer bullets came at us from the ends of each jetty. Since the French were shooting so much from both jetties, the entrance to the port was not accessible for us to go between the jetties. Orders came for us to head toward the beaches just east of the jetties and capture the hills behind the town.

My barge was leaking. I was sitting in water almost up to my shoulders. Pumps were working hard to empty the barge. My fall had shocked me some, and I kept falling asleep as we headed for the shore. When my face hit the water, I would wake up and doze off again. This continued for most of the ride to the shore. Approaching those jetties, French machine gunners who were placed there to prevent entrance to the port fired on us. We reached the beach of Arzeu where we made a successful landing.

I was expected to carry a leg of a multiple machine gun mount as well as a case of 50 cal. ammunition in addition to my own rifle and other equipment. I was one of the first to run off the ramp when it was lowered onto the beach, but I was up to my neck in water.

One of my buddies who was to be last off the barge passed me just as a shell went off in the sand. Shells were exploding all around us. The first rays of dawn helped me find an indentation in the sand. I fell into it with all my equipment, but directly under me I saw the upper part of my buddy who had passed by me, and at my side I saw his feet. "What a relief!" he said. "What do we do now?" I thought that his middle had been blown away, but sand had covered him as I jumped in the sand after him. I still don't know how he got there before I did.

We crawled up the bank toward a road that paralleled the beach. The road was a wide boulevard with an esplanade of palm trees separating two lanes of traffic. People were walking along a sidewalk that separated the road from the beach. A group of men in long flowing gowns were hurrying along the sidewalk. This was our introduction to Arabs who made up much of the population of the city of Arzeu. It was Sunday morning of

Art Goddard

November 8, 1942, when we went ashore in Africa. Church bells were ringing, calling people to early morning mass. Three French girls on bicycles were peddling toward the city when a shell exploded nearby. They jumped off their bicycles so fast to take refuge in the ditch by the road that the bicycles continued to roll on by themselves. This struck us as being funny. Some way to have an introduction to Africa!

Directly in front of us was another road coming from the hills to the south of us. Where this road intersected with the beach boulevard there was an Esso gasoline station. My buddy said, "This can't be Africa. We must be on some kind of maneuvers in the States." We weren't.

Suddenly a plane flew low over the beach, strafing us with machine gun fire. We identified them as British Spitfires, so we did not return their fire. Later we were told that the pilots thought we were German invaders. Fortunately no one was killed, but a couple of our men did receive minor wounds. I guess that I was so covered with sand, I was well protected.

As evening approached, we climbed the hills behind the city and set up machine gun positions. Our 40mm cannon did not reach us for several days. They had been on a different ship. A German Junkers 88 flew low over us, and we opened rifle fire at it since our machine guns were not quite ready. The plane was forced down. This was our first success.

My battery went into position in a small quarry near the top of a hill overlooking the city of Arzeu. We were warned that during the night any movement that we might see over the hill could only be caused by the enemy. French forces fortified the area beyond the hill where we were. They were units of the French Foreign

Legion, and no one knew what they might do. An American engineer battalion settled between us and the bottom of the hill, and they too were ordered to fire at anything that moved above them. They were not told that we were between them and the French, who might be at the top of the hill. All through that night one could hear challenges of "Hi Ho Silver" and, its response, "Away." This was our code for identifying friendly soldiers.

One of my buddies foolishly lit a cigarette even though it was against orders. The light from this could be seen for a great distance, and from then on we didn't dare move out of our quarry. Lying on my stomach on top of some rocks, which seemed to be sticking into me, one of my buddies fell on top of me and stayed there through the night.

The next day I had a deep indentation on my stomach, which did not return to normal for several days. For several years I could feel indentations in my chest and stomach area. The medics found nothing broken when they examined me.

It took about three days for the Allies to secure Arzeu and Oran. When French troops realized that Americans, not British troops had led the attack, they stopped resisting. They surrendered the sea plane base, which had been our primary objective. Nearby at Sidi Bel Abbes, the French Foreign Legion had begun to fight us. They suddenly changed sides and joined us. Most French in Algeria now considered us to be liberators rather than the enemies.

At Arzeu it was more than three days before I could take my helmet off. When I did, it was full of hair. I had lost most of my hair, probably because of the shock from my fall, but I probably would have lost all my hair anyway. It had started to fall out before the war.

　　　　　　　　　　　　　　　　　　Art Goddard

After Arzeu was secured, we were detached from the First Infantry Division and assigned to protect the port of Arzeu with our antiaircraft guns. I was assigned to gun crew number 8. We dug in as well as we could at the quarry on top of the hill. At the foot of the hill was a beautiful large villa under construction in spite of the war. This villa was called "Les Jardins." It belonged to a French colonist who was a wealthy contractor and architect who worked in Oran but lived in Arzeu. The owner and I became good friends while we were there, and after the war we corresponded frequently until the Algerian Revolution confiscated his property and forced his family out of Africa. The family owned land and apartments in France and Spain. He spent the rest of his life in France.

A week after we took Arzeu, we were told that if we were Catholics, we could leave the gun crew on the Sunday and attend mass in the local church. Many of us decided to take advantage of this to get off the gun crew, even though some, including me, were not Catholic.

On that Sunday we arrived at the city square in front of the church only to find that we were an hour early. Nearby was a tavern that was open to customers, so several of us went inside the tavern. I informed my buddies that I didn't drink, but they convinced me that there were some non-alcoholic grape juices available. They ordered one for me, and I found it to be sweet and tasty. I did not know that it was a powerful sweet wine. I ordered a second one for myself just before we went into the church for mass. The last thing I remember about that service was calling out, "Stop the saints from moving around." My buddies had to carry me back to our gun crew. I was very sick and vowed no more drinking.

On Christmas Eve, 1942 in Arzeu, one of my buddies and I sneaked into town even though it was off limits for us to buy a Christmas gift for the seven-year-old daughter of the owner of the villa. This was symbolic of our feelings about Christmas since we could not be with our families. Several other members of the gun crew gave us money toward the gift, which we bought and placed on the doorstep of the villa. Although the family was wealthy, they had not been able to make purchases for Christmas. The family was delighted! I soon discovered that this family was very influential among the French living in the area, and their appreciation for what we did helped us with the people of Arzeu.

That Christmas was a very lonely one for us. We had not received any mail since our landing. We had been promised a Thanksgiving dinner, but we had to settle for a couple rabbits that some of the men had caught along with our usual c-rations.

We had been promised a banquet for Christmas, but as darkness descended on Christmas Eve, we had nothing. It rained hard, and our morale was very low. There wasn't a star visible in the sky. The wind was blowing off the Mediterranean Sea, and it was very cold. About an hour before midnight we heard band music playing Christmas carols rising from the jetties where machine guns had been. As the music started the rain stopped, the clouds cleared, and we could see the stars and a beautiful full moon. A truck arrived with mail and many Christmas packages. Another truck arrived with ingredients for a full Christmas dinner. We were overcome with emotion. I was greatly pleased that our army thought enough about us to give us a Christmas so far away from our homes. Many of us thought, however, that this would be our last Christmas.

Shortly after Christmas we were placed under a

major alert. All our guard positions were doubled. The French Admiral Darlan, who was the number two man in the Vichy French government, had been assassinated in Algiers. We were not allowed to leave our position, but on New Year's Day I received word that one of my buddies and I were to go to a certain address in downtown Arzeu for dinner. There we found that the owner of the villa near our positions had pulled strings through French military to get us released so that we could spend the day with them. We had a wonderful New Year's dinner with the family.

After the war, I received a letter from the family in Arzeu that the people had chosen the quarry where we had scratched our names into the rock as their World War II memorial. Since the Algerian Revolution, I wonder if it is still there.

During our stay at Arzeu, we sometimes became stressed with boredom. One of our men had an attack of appendicitis and died during surgery. Battery B of our battalion was ordered to the front. The rest of us continued anti-aircraft protection for the ports of Arzeu and Oran. One evening we joined with the French in Oran for a major celebration for their liberation from the Nazis. This was the only entertainment we had there.

By March 1943 we were reassigned to the First Infantry Division and headed for the front line, which was now in Tunisia. American forces had been stopped at Kassarine Pass, which was an entrance from Algeria into Tunisia. Reinforcements were called up to go to the aid of the hard pressed Allies there. On our way we bivouacked outside of Algiers. Because there were so many Arabs there, we tripled our guard, forming a circle like in the old west. We knew that many of these Arabs were successful and clever thieves. Most of us slept either on the ground or under a truck, but one of our lieutenants insisted that an army cot would be put up for him in the middle of the camp. He felt he would be quite safe there, but he was wrong. All of a sudden he shrieked. His shoes had been taken right off his feet. He had no other shoes, and the size of his feet was too large for immediate replacement. He had to go for days wearing rope sandals as many of the local natives did. During that night some of our men lost blankets, which the Arabs pulled off them while they slept. Replacement supplies were not plentiful.

As we traveled farther east along the coastal area, we were partially blocked by peaks of the Atlas Mountains.

My battery platoon became separated from the other platoon. Instead of going around some of the high mountains, we found a road that went over them. It was a very narrow and dangerous road with steep cliffs on one side and many curves so sharp that we had to disconnect our guns and trailers and man handle them around the curve. Our route was half the distance it would have been if we had gone around the mountain.

We actually reached the other side of the mountain about the same time that the first platoon did. We shoved on toward Kassarine Pass where our forces had been shoved back by German troops under Rommel. General Terry Allen had been replaced by General George Patton as our new commander. Patton led another tank battle, and this time we won. It was widely reported that General Patton had stated that he had read the same books as Field Marshall Rommel, and therefore knew his plans. Our troops contacted the British 8th Army under British General Montgomery, and aided by French forces we continued to drive the Germans and Italians out of

Tunisia. Italian troops had remained behind to hold the Allies back to give the Germans time to evacuate. They remained in the vicinity of Cape Bon. During this time I was involved in considerable ground fighting and air attacks.

With the capture of the city of Tunis and nearby Cape Bon, Axis fighting in North Africa came to an end. We were stationed on Cape Bon for several days. The beaches near us were very clear, and sugar white sand invited us into the surf. Although our engineers had cleared the beaches of mines, we were ordered not to go into the water. The temperature was around 120 degrees, and some of us couldn't resist going into the water anyway.

We didn't stay in long because pieces of bodies and uniforms floated among us. The Germans had tried to withdraw their troops in their own "Dunkirk" evacuation. They had not been successful.

On Cape Bon we pitched our pup tents in an apricot orchard. There were so many fresh apricots hanging from the tress that we could simply reach up from our prone position in our pup tent and pick some. We remained on Cape Bon for a few days. Since we had been in continuous combat for some time, we were sent to a rest camp, which was only a few miles from the city of Tunis.

One day while there, I wrote a letter home complaining that a college degree and even a master's degree didn't seem to mean much in the army. I had been promoted to a PFC, but that was all. The battery adjutant censured my letter, and I was called to battalion headquarters. The colonel promoted me to a T5 rank as mail orderly for Battery D. We had no battery clerk, so I was assigned his duties too. I was unwilling to leave my buddies on the gun crew, but I finally moved into battery headquarters. It was my choice.

Because I could speak French, I was given the assignment to go to the public market in Tunis and buy fresh fruits and vegetables. The market began at sunrise, so I left with a jeep and driver and also a three quarter ton truck each morning for Tunis. As soon as we filled the truck, I sent it back to camp and the jeep driver and I remained in Tunis for several hours. The American Red Cross occupied a large hotel in the center of the city. It was air-conditioned, so my driver and I spent much time there. The Red Cross provided coffee and donuts too, but we had to pay for them. We took sightseeing trips around the city, including one to neighboring Carthage.

Not only were the ruins of the ancient city interesting, but it was also the home of the Bey of Tunis. It was a spectacular sight to watch the changing of guard ceremony at the Bey's palace. I hadn't realized that the ruins of Carthage were not of the original city but of a Roman replacement of it.

When I was in Tunis, I had met a Moslem priest who invited me to his home for a meal. He said that it was a holy day for him. The meal consisted of black bread, a bowl of olive oil, and an orange. There was a cup of green tea to drink too. I was expected to dunk the bread into the olive oil and then eat it. The more oil that dripped down my chin, the more it meant that I appreciated the meal. I'm afraid the meal was not appealing, but I did appreciate the cleric's kindness.

I also met a Turkish family while I was at the market. They owned a store in Tunis and lived in the Kasbah section of the city. They invited me to dinner at their home. Since it was off limits for me to go into the Kasbah, they gave me an Arab cloak to cover my uniform. They bound my head with a towel, and escorted me to their beautiful home in the center of the Kasbah. This was a great experience, and the meal was very good too. I may have broken rules, but it was worth it.

The city of Tunis celebrated for the second time its liberation from German control on Bastille Day in 1943. There was a grand parade and much celebration throughout the day. My buddies and I continued to enjoy the comfort of the air-conditioned hotel lobby.

From Tunis we worked our way to the coastal city of Bizerte, Tunisia. One night as I was pulling guard duty, I fell into my own fox hole, sprained my ankle, and was given limited duty for a couple of days.

Meanwhile the war was going on as the U. S. Seventh Army invaded Sicily on its southern beaches while the British Eighth Army invaded on the eastern coastal area. Husky was the code name given to the Allied invasion of Sicily. After the original landings by the Allies, my battalion prepared to leave Africa on a LST from the port of Bizerte. We were attached to the Third Division under General Truscott.

Arriving at the port of Bizerte, we experienced a serious air raid at dark. It was frustrating for us because our anti-aircraft guns were packed for movement to Sicily. I spent most of the duration of the air raid exposed to falling shrapnel as I had carelessly placed the metal part of my helmet on a truck. In spite of the danger, I was amused when a bomb exploded nearby. Several of my buddies and also officers jumped into a ditch we had just dug as a latrine ditch. They were messed up, but it saved them from being hit. I remained under the truck where I had left my helmet and did not receive a scratch. The next day we sailed from Bizerte for Sicily.

CHAPTER 4

HUSKY

Husky was the code name for the invasion of Sicily. It was a joint invasion by the British Eighth Army under General Montgomery and the American Seventh Army under General Patton. The plan was for the British to invade Sicily on its eastern coast near the cities of Syracuse, Augusta, and Catania, and then shove north to Messina. American forces were to land on the south beaches near the cities of Gela and Licata. American forces were to drive northeasterly through the rugged mountains and meet up with the British at Messina. General Patton thought it would hasten the capture of the island by landing in the northwest corner of the island near the city of Palermo. The British didn't approve of the Palermo landings because they wanted to reach Messina first. At least, this is what General Patton was reported as saying. There was considerable rivalry between the two generals.

Arriving at Bizerte, the 431st boarded a LST transport. LST stood for landing ship tank, which was a flat bottom ship with gang planks that could be lowered so that vehicles, including tanks, could drive out onto a dock or a beach. This ship bounced around a great deal and many of my buddies became sick, but once again, I did not. As part of the Third Division we were under General Truscott, its commander.

General Patton was convinced that a Palermo landing was necessary for our success, so the city had been taken shortly before we arrived.

We were able to unload at the docks with most of our equipment. We remained a few days near Palermo where the citizens treated us joyfully.

We enjoyed some sightseeing while we were in Palermo. I visited a beautiful cathedral in the suburb city of Monreale. There were pillars with mosaic pictures depicting the life of Christ. Some of these mosaics contained precious jewels and stones, and to keep the stones from thieves, iron bars had been constructed more than an arm's length away from the pillars. One could see the pillars only through slits between the bars. Beneath that church was an extensive catacomb that I was able to visit. I was escorted by a monk who delighted in telling stories about the bodies that were there. I remember well the coffin in which a young girl had been preserved for hundreds of years. There was a glass cover over the coffin, and I could see color in her cheeks. The monk informed me that the Palermo catacombs were surpassed only by those in Rome.

In the meantime British troops succeeded in landing on the east coast, and they were advancing toward Catania, which is the second largest city in Sicily. When American troops landed on the south coast, paratroopers were to land behind the lines in order to capture defense positions from the rear. Under the cover of darkness, some of the planes missed their targets due to very heavy winds. Some of these planes flew over the convoy carrying American ground troops. The convoy was escorted by British ships, and on one ship a British observer thought the planes flying over them were Germans. Antiaircraft fire now sent our planes scattering. This caused great confusion. In spite of these problems, we took Gela and Licata.

When we left Palermo, we drove east along a road close to the coast. Mountains rose steeply south of the road, and on the north side of the road were steep cliffs. Swift flowing streams descended out of the mountains and over the cliffs into the sea.

There were partially destroyed bridges over gullies where parts of the road had been washed away or bombed. American engineers worked very hard to restore the roads so that they could be used.

As we progressed closer to Messina, many Italian soldiers surrendered to us. Many Italians had relatives in the U.S. Army and they did not want to fight us. Although we did not know it yet, Mussolini had been replaced by Badoglio as premier of Italy. Mussolini was aided by German and Italian fascists to escape and continue leading Italian forces in the northern part of Italy. German troops, however, still had to be driven out of Sicily and southern Italy.

The road we were on was very narrow with steep hills on the south and steep cliffs on the north. The hills to the south were blazing with fires started by flame throwers as our troops tried to flush out the enemy. There were piles of bodies stacked along the side of the road waiting for ambulances or trucks to carry them off. The odor of dead and burning flesh was terrible.

That day, as night was falling, our battalion commander ordered the 431st to bivouac in a narrow and very muddy hillside. It was apparent to us that our vehicles would be stuck in the mud and become "sitting ducks" if the Germans attacked us from the air. I was riding in the jeep with the captain of Battery D when he received the orders to pull into that field of mud. He was very angry and ordered our jeep driver to pull to the front of the convoy so that he could confront the colonel.

When we reached the colonel, we found that the commanders of all the other batteries were there. The major who was second in command was arguing with the colonel. The captains of the other batteries were supporting the major in this argument.

With his hand on his revolver, I heard the colonel order that all officers must follow his orders or he would shoot them. About this time we saw a jeep coming along the road toward us. It was darting in and out around our vehicles and was flying a flag with three stars. We knew that General Patton had arrived.

General Patton stopped near me and jumped out of his jeep, shouting at me in a rather high squeaky voice, "Who is in charge of this g-d—n gypsy caravan?" I saluted and pointed to the colonel calling him by name. General Patton rushed up to the colonel and asked," Did you order these vehicles into that g-d—n field?" The colonel admitted that he did. Patton then turned to the major and asked, "Did you approve of this mess?" The major replied, "No." Patton then turned to the colonel and said, "Lieutenant, report to the rear for reclassification." Then he turned to the major and said, "Colonel, you are now in charge." The former colonel had confiscated a Chevrolet sedan in Palermo that he was using as his command car. Patton now turned to me and said, "Soldier, get some men and throw that g-d—n car over the cliff." We willingly obeyed.

After working hard to get the stuck vehicles free from the mud, we drove on to find a better place for the night. Vehicles in convoy at night are not allowed to have their lights on when they are in a combat area. Each vehicle had a reflector that was the only visible light to guide by.

That night one of our trucks broke down and blocked the road, so the last seven vehicles of the convoy could not get by. I was riding in the first truck behind the one that had broken down. The rest of the convoy pulled out of sight. Finally we fixed the truck and hastened on to catch the convoy.

The other trucks were out of sight, but we sped up trying to reach them. We passed one of our buddies standing on the side of the road where a narrow dirt road descended to the beach. He waved at us as we passed him.

The quantity of burning vehicles and fires on the hillside was increasing. Suddenly some infantry men jumped in front of us and ordered us to stop. They asked where we were going. I informed them that we were trying to catch up with the vehicle that had just turned a corner because it must be our convoy. The infantry men said that it was a retreating German tank. We had reached the front all right, but now we had to turn around and go back to find the rest of the battalion.

We unfastened the guns that we were pulling and man-handled them to turn around on that narrow road as our trucks turned around too. We wanted to get out of there as soon as possible. We drove back to where we had passed our buddy who waved at us. He was still there. When we reached him, he told us that he had tried to tell us to go down the narrow road to the beach, which was where the others were.

When we reached the water's edge, it was very dark, but I could make out shapes of trucks and men in the night. Orders were for us to dig fox holes. My buddy Gazza, who along with the rest of my battery had already dug in, called to me saying that his fox hole was big enough for two. Following the sound of his voice, I saw the edge of the fox hole and jumped in. I soon fell asleep leaning against the side of the fox hole.

As dawn arrived, I saw Gazza's head just a few feet beyond me. We were not in the same fox hole, but someone was there with me. I turned around and discovered that I had spent the night with a dead German soldier.

I took an armband and a souvenir ring of the Siegfried Line from him. These are among the few souvenirs I brought back from the War.

A special task force was organized to make a behind the lines landing near the town of Brolo. An LST took us as infantry to the beach near the town. We realized that we were behind German and Italian lines. The only food we had was the emergency chocolate bar that all soldiers carried at all times. There was a vineyard nearby and many of us picked grapes to go along with the chocolate. This was a mistake as the grapes had been spayed with something that made us ill.

Although we were behind Axis lines, Italian troops were there and tried to surrender to us. There was no way we could take prisoners, and they did not want to take us as prisoners. We were cut off by the Germans and could not advance from the beach. We just waited for the main forces of the 3rd Division to come to our aid. We were there a couple of days before we were rescued. I had

Art Goddard

always thought that General Truscott was responsible for our eventual relief, but when I saw the movie "Patton," I realized that it was Patton who made the forces break through to relieve us.

General Patton was known for his very strict uniform regulations. All men had to wear the dress uniform when we were in combat. It was very hot in Sicily, with temperatures frequently above 100 degrees. If anyone was caught out of uniform by the MPs, not only was the soldier punished, but his commanding officer was too. Such a penalty was usually a fine and a reduction in rank.

One of my pup tent mates in Sicily was a sergeant who was rather unusual. If bugs bothered him, he would light matches to burn them. He often kept me awake at night as he searched for bugs to burn.

This sergeant bitterly resented the uniform regulations and violated them any chance he had. One day as he was washing his feet in his steel helmet because he had a bad heat rash, some MPs caught him. He lost all of his stripes and our battery commander was fined fifty dollars. My captain told me to see that the sergeant was assigned the next hazardous duty to come along. He survived the war, but I had a different pup tent mate after that.

We were in Sicily at the time of the famous "slapping" event involving General Patton. The General was visiting the wounded in field hospitals when he came upon a healthy looking soldier. Without trying to find out what was wrong with the soldier, Patton accused him of being a coward and slapped him. The soldier was suffering from battle fatigue and shock. Medical authorities reported this episode to higher command, and soon General Patton was recalled and General Patch took his place as commander of the Seventh Army. Patton was censured by our government but was allowed to continue later as commander of our Third Army.

As the fighting was ending in Sicily, Patton and his men reached Messina before the British under Montgomery did. Montgomery thought that he had reached Messina first, but in the center of the city he found Patton waiting for him. It is doubtful that Montgomery ever forgave Patton for this.

When the fighting ended in Sicily, my battalion was sent to a resort area for rest and recovery. This was near the city of Agrigento. We were billeted in a small hotel on the beach nearby. Each morning we had to go swimming and also do infantry drills, but otherwise we were free to visit the ancient ruins of Agrigento.

Greek and Roman ruins of several temples, which had been built to honor their god and goddesses, dominated the hills around the city. Some of these temples were in remarkably good condition even though they were thousands of years old.

Following a few days of rest, we set up anti-aircraft positions in towns such as Menfi, Sciacca, and Castelvetrano along the southern coast. There were landing fields near these port cities. One day we received orders not to fire on any Italian planes that might try to land on one of the fields. Several planes did land. We learned that Italy had surrendered and many Italian troops were actually joining us to fight against the Germans.

One day as I was standing near a 40mm cannon watching bombers take off from the runway, one plane crashed as it took off and exploded several yards from me. Although I dropped to the ground, some debris bounced off the ground and hit me in the face. Fortunately whatever struck me had lost most of its momentum. I was sent to the field hospital where they patched me up quickly and removed the rest of my teeth. I was sent back to my battery on limited duty for a week and then reported back to the hospital. The hospital dentists made impressions of my gum and fitted me with new teeth. I still have those teeth after sixty years of service. Unfortunately, I was not able to claim a purple heart for the injury. Italy had surrendered and where it happened was considered to be a non combat area. I would have received five more points toward discharge, but I had more than enough without them.

Shortly after returning to full duty, there was a serious epidemic of hepatitis, and I was very ill. I was back in the hospital again, this time in Castelvetrano, Sicily.

After much medication and an enjoyable diet of roasts, potatoes, pies, cakes and candy, I recovered and returned to my battery. Upon leaving the hospital, I was told never to give blood. Nearly seventy percent of my battery had the disease, and for several days we were considered to be non-combat. During this time, preparations were being made for an invasion of the Italian mainland.

British forces under General Montgomery had crossed the Strait of Messina and were gradually moving up the Italian peninsula along the Adriatic Coast. U. S. forces under General Mark Clark landed at Salerno on Italy's west coast. The port of Naples was captured by American forces and rapidly restored. Its docks were now available for American and British forces to bring supplies. Our troops began to drive north through the Apennine Mountains, which were very rugged and well defended by the Germans. Heavy rains swelled the rivers so that movement through the valleys was slow and dangerous, and sometimes impossible.

There was a mountain from which one could control movement to the north through the valleys below. On top of the mountain called Mount Casino was a famous monastery filled with religious and historical treasures. German troops surrounded the area and would not surrender even when we shelled it and tried to drive them off with infantry attacks. U.S.troops realized that we would have no choice but to bomb the area, but we did not want to destroy the monastery. A major attempt was made to bypass the area by a landing behind the lines at Anzio, which lay between Casino and Rome. This invasion was not successful at first because many German reinforcements were present. The battle for Anzio turned out to be one of the bloodiest of the entire war. German strength was so great that we had to bomb Mount Casino.

After this, U. S. troops finally broke through and were on their way to Rome, which they entered about the same time as the Allied invasion of Normandy.

I was still in Sicily with the 3rd Division when the attack at Anzio took place. The 3rd Division had a major part in that battle and many troops were lost. My battalion was in Palermo, preparing to board an LST bound for Anzio, when a messenger arrived with orders that detached us from the 3rd Division We were assigned to protect landing fields on the island of Sardinia. Our chaplain, supply sergeant, and a few others had already boarded the LST and did go to Anzio. We learned later that they were all killed during the landing. I thought that there but for the grace of God I would have died too.

At Palermo there was a captured Italian light cruiser, the "Montecucullo," which was being used as a troop transport. We boarded that ship and sailed for Sardinia.

CHAPTER 5

SARDINIA AND CORSICA

The ship taking us from Palermo to Sardinia was overcrowded. There wasn't enough room to stretch out and be comfortable anywhere on board. The food consisted of C rations, but some of the ship's crew had obtained access to the officer's pantry and made small apricot pies that they sold to us for ten dollars each. The pies were good, but the black market was very active in many ways on board the ship.

The trip on the cruiser was smooth and fast. When we reached the port of Cagliari, Sardinia, the capital and largest city of the island, we transferred from the ship to fishing boats that took us to a dock. Our trucks and guns had been loaded on a freighter and arrived several days later. Borrowed trucks took us to the town of Villacidro where we waited for our guns, and then we went on to the town of Castelvetrano. We went into antiaircraft positions to guard a large airfield there. An Italian search light battalion was already there, and it was attached to us. We were told to dig in and prepare for an extended stay. It was November 1943 when we reached Sardinia, and we didn't leave until July 1944. The war was passing us by.

At first we lived in pup tents, but later we set up larger tents. There was very little need for antiaircraft. The only enemy planes that flew over were observation planes, and they were so high that they were beyond the reach of our guns. There was no need for infantry, and the civilians were friendly.

In our larger tents the army provided cots for us. A small, well built tent served as our battery headquarters, and a much larger tent was our mess hall. We also had a trailer where our radio and other communications material were kept.

As spring arrived, the weather became unbearably hot. Some of us pooled some money, and for about 100 dollars hired local civilians to build adobe style huts for us.

Each hut was large enough for five soldiers, cots, luggage, and a table. One day a French squadron of fighter planes landed on our field. It was the Esquadille Lafayette, one of France's best. With the French troops, the Italian searchlight battalion, and natives speaking Sardo, I had to make good use of my knowledge of languages. This plus other duties as battery clerk and mail orderly kept me busy most of the time.

One day the first sergeant of my battery and some other soldiers found an unexploded bomb. They recognized it as a fire bomb. They decided to take the bomb to the top of a nearby three story shed and drop it to see if it would explode. They dropped the bomb, and it did explode but did no damage to the building although it continued to burn. The sergeant and the men rushed down the stairs and approached the burning bomb. I called out to them to watch out because there could be a booby trap inside. The Germans were noted for putting antipersonnel bombs inside other types. I was correct. The bomb exploded again, slightly injuring a couple of soldiers including the first sergeant. The first sergeant's injuries were so severe that from then on he had limited duty and made frequent visits to hospitals for treatment. His injuries, however, were not serious enough to allow him to be sent home and discharged. The battalion officers decided to keep him as an official first sergeant, but I was made acting first sergeant. I had already been doing most of the clerical work of the first sergeant as well as my duties as mail orderly. From then on I was sort of in charge, but I couldn't wear the stripes or receive the pay because the first sergeant was still on the table of organization.

This suited me except that I wished I had the pay. Later on I was given a medal for this double duty.

There were some benefits to being a first sergeant that I enjoyed. Since I made our guard rosters, I didn't have to serve guard duty. From time to time I did assign myself that duty anyway. I was also assigned to accompany the captain when he visited various gun positions, etc. It was also expected that I would visit all of our men who were hospitalized, deliver the mail, pick up PX rations, etc. One duty was assigned that I did not like. The captain ordered me to censor the mail. Some of my buddies had so many personal problems that I did not see how they could go on. I realized that I was in a position to advise and help them. I did whatever I could. Since we had no chaplain, I apparently was filling that position too. I found reward in the confidence and respect that the men had for me.

Another advantage as first sergeant was that I could have a jeep and driver when I wanted one. The lieutenant in charge of our second platoon enjoyed exploring the island, and he and I found many interesting places to explore together.

One time we found a very steep hill on top of which were the ruins of a medieval castle called Sequoia. Among the ruins of this castle were walls that were in fair condition and a dungeon.

While climbing among the ruins, I found some old coins identified as Maltese coins. Unfortunately the coins were in my barracks bag of souvenirs that were stolen from me later.

Sardinia had many unusual stone structures that, perhaps, dated from the Stone Age. Natives called some of the structures "nurogi." They were spirals with hollow walls containing steps that led to the top peak of the spiral. There was a platform at the peak. Probably these were built by sun worshipers. The platform seemed to be like an altar facing the rising sun. In modern times most of these structures were being used as a home for shepherds who inhabited the land.

Most of the land of Sardinia seemed to be too poor for successful agricultural use. Some of the very barren parts of west Texas that I have seen remind me of Sardinia. One day while the lieutenant and I were exploring, we came upon a narrow road that was parallel to a little brook. The brook and road seemed to come out of a grotto. We followed the road through the grotto and entered an entirely different world. The fields were green, corn was ripe in its stalks, and good looking fresh vegetables filled the gardens. There were a few very well kept farm houses that we recognized as having modern utilities. We had stumbled upon an experimental farm

Art Goddard

that Mussolini had bragged would restore the island as a fruitful place. I understand that since the war, much of Sardinia has been reclaimed and is now a prosperous tourist resort, especially for the wealthy.

One of my duties as mail orderly required me to travel twice each week to the port Cagliari.

The roads of Sardinia were so bad that anyone who traveled any distance was required to report to the medics for a back massage after each trip. I looked forward to that after each trip, which was about 100 miles round trip from our base.

As barren and poor as the island appeared, a railroad ran from Cagliari to Sassari, Sardinia's second largest city. Each day a modern stream train raced along those rails. Natives carried supplies on their backs, pulled goods in donkey trucks, and trudged through muddy roads that paralleled the railroad. Women balanced baskets of supplies on their heads while men simply walked along behind them. The contrast was astounding.

Most of us in Sardinia found a family that would wash and iron our clothes. Twice each week, a five year old girl came to our camp and picked up or returned a bag of laundry. The clothes came back clean, ironed, and smelled nice. All of this cost only a nickel. I usually gave more than that and a candy bar as well if I had one.

The Italian searchlight battalion that was attached to us was already in action when we arrived. The Italian soldiers were very friendly and easy for us to deal with, when it was necessary. Many of the soldiers in my battery were of Italian descent, and some found a relative among the Italian soldiers.

I had studied Italian in college and could communicate with many, but there were so many dialects that I found it difficult. One of my buddies who was not Italian enjoyed socializing with them and frequently joined them in drinking parties. This buddy was seldom sober. One morning he missed roll call, but I found him with the Italians conversing as if he spoke their language. He was very gifted in languages.

This buddy was assigned to the communications sergeant who arranged for him to attend a two week course in the Morse code. He returned the next day having mastered everything about the code in one day.

June 6, 1944, known as D-Day, when Allied forces landed in Normandy, saw us still on the island.

We listened to BBC radio reports of progress being made and wondered when we would get off Sardinia and join the front line again. We felt frustrated and forgotten. One of my officers tried to comfort us by saying, "We who only sit and wait also serve." We were very tired of waiting.

Early in July we heard rumors of preparations for another landing in Southern France. We received orders to leave Sardinia. Our trucks took us to the north coast of the island near the Strait of Bonafaccio. We waited for barges to take us across the strait to the southern coast of Corsica. Children from nearby villages came to our camp to beg for food. They were starving. We had to surround our camp with armed guards. Children tried many ways to reach our mess truck and kitchen areas. At breakfast we had the usual lumpy and slimy oatmeal, tasteless powdered eggs, and a thick green coffee that most of us could not drink. We often threw the greater part of our meal into the garbage can. While we were trying to eat, children dug into our garbage ditch. They scooped out food to take home to their families. We had not witnessed such starvation in southern Sardinia. We were very sad for the natives and threw whatever food we could over the fence that we had built so that they could get it and take the food home.

It only took a few hours to cross from Sardinia to Corsica. It was a beautiful day, the sea was smooth, and everything worked like clockwork. We finally left Sardinia and now were on the south coast of the island of Corsica.

After the successful landing, we drove by convoy north along the east coast of the island to the city of Bastia. When we reached Bastia, we discovered that we were to have gone north on the west coast to the town of Propriano, so we did and then encamped for several days.

During the time we were in Sardinia we had not been very active. We had become soft and needed infantry type drills to toughen us up again. Rumors abounded that we were about to invade Southern France, and we needed to prepare for that invasion.

There was confusion over the code name for the coming invasion of Southern France. Prime Minister Winston Churchill of England wanted the Allied invasion to be from the Adriatic Sea and go north through Yugoslavia into Poland, and thus cut off Russian troops from reaching Germany first. American military insisted upon invading Southern France. Then the plan was to travel up the Rhone River Valley, cross through Alsace to the Rhine River and into Germany. The invasion took place in Southern France and was called "Anvil" until we were well established. The name was changed to "Dragoon," which was what the British wanted. Apparently this name change pleased Churchill.

Upon completing a couple weeks of infantry drills near Propriano, we moved into the port city of Ajaccio, capital of Corsica. On August 15, 1944, Allied forces of the Seventh Army successfully invaded Southern France, but we were left out. The LST that we were to board had been sunk before it reached port Ajaccio, and my battery was ordered to remain in Ajaccio until a replacement arrived. We spent several days in that city before an LST arrived.

The U.S. Seventh Army was now under the command of General Patch. Patton had been relieved of his command because of his conduct in Sicily. While we were in Ajaccio, I saw much of the city. Napoleon had been born there, and I visited the house where he had lived. I was impressed with his small cradle. I took my boot off and my foot didn't quite fit into the cradle. What a small baby he must have been, but he certainly became a famous French leader.

When our LST finally arrived, we boarded it in spite of a severe storm plowing through the Mediterranean.

CHAPTER 6

DRAGOON

We left Ajaccio, Corsica on an LST without escort. Allied forces had already landed in Southern France. We did not know where we were to go. Although the journey was not far, it was very dangerous that day because of a severe storm with hurricane force. Our flat bottom LST rocked from side to side and from bow to stern. Most of our men and many of the ship's crew were seasick, but I was not. I was terrified and feared that the ship would roll over at any moment. I fastened my arms around the inside rail on the deck surrounding the entrance to the crew's quarters; I stayed there hanging on for most of the trip.

Some of the men were in the hold of the ship lying under the cargo elevator. The elevator was used to raise trucks, guns, and supplies from the hold to the deck. The elevator broke loose and slowly began to descend on the men, who quickly scrambled safely out of harm's way.

Shortly after we were out of sight of land, an

announcement was made over the loud speakers that we were heading for the French city of Marsailles, which had been recently occupied by U. S. troops. The announcement continued, however, saying that we were being blown off course and were heading to the Axis seaport city of Genoa, Italy. We were reminded to give only our name, rank, and serial number if we were captured. To our relief another announcement was made stating that we were heading to the French seaport city of Toulon.

The storm was getting worse. A sailor came out from the crew quarters carrying an orange crate. He broke off a side of it and started to whittle the wood down to a certain measurement. I asked him what he was doing, and he replied, "We have a little leak in the seams that needs patching."

We who were on deck looked at each other in silence, but we were expecting the worst. Soon the sailor came back with a much larger piece of wood and, aided by other sailors, cut it so that it would plug a larger hole. A short time after the sailors went inside, they returned with the leg of a mess hall table and started cutting it down to size. I heard one sailor say to the others that he hoped the leg was going to fix it, but he told them all to keep their life belts on.

I was still frozen to the rail that I had been hanging on to when a cry rang out,"Land!" We entered the harbor of Toulon safely. In 1942 when the Allies invaded French North Africa, the French had scuttled their ships that were based at Toulon. They did this so that that the Germans could not use them and also to prevent the Allies from bombing them. The British had bombed the French fleet that was at the port of Oran at the time of the Nazi takeover of France in 1940. At that time there had been much damage to civilian buildings, and the French didn't want a repetition.

We slowly sailed over the submerged ships. We could look down over the side of our ship and see the masts, funnels, decks, etc. of the scuttled ships. It was an awesome sight! Hoping that we could disembark at Toulon and proceed by trucks to Marseilles, some of our officers went ashore to try to make such arrangements. They returned shortly to report that we were to continue by LST to Marsailles in spite of the storm. As we sailed out of the port of Toulon, the sea was quieting down. The storm was over. We sailed close to the shore until we finally entered the harbor of Marsailles. When we got off the LST, we marched through the streets of the city to a camp ground north of the city. We pitched our tents, mostly pup tents.

We remained in Marsailles a few days repairing damage done to some of our vehicles by the storm. It was there that my cousin Wally, who was stationed in the Port Authority at Marsailles, visited me. He had learned that my battery had arrived, and he obtained a pass to visit me. He stayed so late that he had to spend the night. After the war, he confessed that he had gone AWOL because he overstayed his pass time. As a result he had lost his stripes. He said that the visit was worth it anyway.

The Germans were retreating north through the Rhone Valley. We were in pursuit of them, but they were hard to reach. As we followed the retreating Germans we went through several cities that I had studied, such as Avignon, Orange, and Dijon. Near Dijon, heavy rains had caused the Rhone River to overflow. The flooding slowed down our advance. Although the Allied invasion of Southern France had been on August 15, 1944, it was September before we caught up with the Germans.

We were part of the Seventh Army under General

Patch, who had replaced Patton after his "slapping" episode. We were now assigned to the 100th Division task force, which was to chase the Germans northwardly up the valley of the Rhone River, through the Vosges Mountains, and then east to the Rhine River. Our destination was to take the province of Alsace and reach the city of Strasbourg on the Rhine River. Germany would be just across the Rhine.

We had to fight as infantry as we pushed through the Vosges Mountains into Alsace. Germans had to be flushed out of hills, forests, and small towns as we progressed.

Some places were easy to take as the French underground cleaned out the Germans before we reached them. Often, however, snipers remained behind. Sniper fire did hit some of our men, but no one was killed.

One night, because I spoke French, a lieutenant and I were ordered to go behind the German lines to a farmhouse where we would meet some French underground soldiers. We made it to the farmhouse by crawling through muddy marshes and a swampy forest. After a brief discussion about how the French could help our advance, we returned to our lines. We encountered a squad of Germans who were probably looking for us, but we successfully defeated them in a brief battle. I must have shot four or five myself, but I don't like to remember this. The rest we captured and turned over to the nearby French soldiers for further questioning. Neither the lieutenant nor I were injured, but we were covered with mud and soaking wet from a swamp where we had hid. It was after two o'clock in the morning when we finally reached our lines, exhausted and very dirty.

In one of the small villages that we took, some women were holding a young girl while one of them cut

Art Goddard

off her hair. The girl broke away from the women and ran into the woods nearby. We learned that this was the way the citizens treated anyone who collaborated with the Germans willingly.

The 100th Infantry Division task force was attempting to break through the Vosges Mountains onto the plains of Alsace. In Alsace my knowledge of French and German proved again to be very useful. With the aid of French forces we reached the city of Strasbourg, which we captured with very little resistance.

The Germans had withdrawn from the city so rapidly that they had left electric power on. Trolley cars were actually running. We chose a small inn for our battery headquarters in the outskirts of the city. There was a refrigerator in the kitchen that had an icemaker. What a treat it was to have a good cold glass of water. That night the Germans shelled power plants and generators and all electric power was destroyed.

We sent patrols out north and west of the city to try to wipe out any German units that might still be in the area. The French had built a strong line of defense called the Maginot Line to keep the Germans out of France. It ran from the border of Switzerland on the west side of the German border to the Belgian border. It was believed to be impenetrable. Because of this the Germans had built a line of defense on their side of the border to keep the French out. The German line was called the Siegfried Line, or the West Wall. These defense positions were very well built and both sides believed they would save them from invading forces. In 1940, however, German armies had simply entered France from the north by violating the neutrality of Belgium as they had done during World War I. The Maginot Line did not help the French at all, and France surrendered in 1940. When we were in that area, we experimented with guns at our disposal to see which ones could penetrate these defense positions. Our 40mm guns, using armor piercing shells, simply threw a few chips and dirt about when it hit on both defense lines. The 105mm Howitzer made a hole in a Maginot Line "pill boxes," but it just bounced off the Siegfried Line pill boxes. The 155mm Long Tom gun destroyed the Maginot Line position, but not the Siegfried Line. It took the 8 inch howitzer cannon and the 240mm cannon to destroy the Siegfried pill boxes. This made us realize that it would be a long time before we could defeat Germany.

One day while we were near Strasbourg, we made our headquarters in a large inn. That night, for the first time in weeks, I was able to sleep in a bed with clean sheets. In the middle of the night our sleep was interrupted by a terrific explosion, and the concussion from it knocked me out of the bed. A 240mm gun had gone into position about a mile away. The gun started to shell positions on the Siegfried Line. German artillery began to shell us to destroy that one cannon. We had to take refuge in shell holes for the rest of the night.

The Germans had developed a very fast plane using jet engines. One day one of those planes flew over us and dropped a bomb, landing about fifty feet from where I was standing. It did not explode, as it turned out to be a dud. Increasingly German artillery was shooting shells that did not explode. The plane that had tried to bomb us was actually after the 240mm gun position about two miles beyond us. That showed us that jet bombers were not very accurate, at least at that time.

On another day a lieutenant and I were returning from a scouting mission when ME109s strafed us. We took refuge in a drainage ditch beside the road. Although our jeep received several bullet holes, we were not hit. This was another narrow escape for me.

In December 1944, the Germans launched an all out effort to drive the Allies back to the sea. The resulting battles became known as "The Battle of the Bulge." Our 431ˢᵗ Battalion was not involved with this battle, but we did experience a minor effort on the part of the Germans where we were. Apparently the Germans tried to deceive the Allies about the intended area they were to attack. The Germans did try to shove us out of the Strasbourg area, but their efforts were not serious there. Their real plan was to drive our armies back through Belgium and take the seaport city of Antwerp. This would not only give them access to the sea, but would drive a wedge between the British and American forces. From time to time German planes strafed us, but did not drop many bombs.

We set up our antiaircraft positions near the Corps Headquarters in Alsace. One day a squadron of P51s flew over us and dropped bombs and strafed our positions. Since they were our planes, we thought that the pilots believed that we were Germans. Prearranged signals were used to identify us as Americans, but the planes circled around and came at us again. This time one of the bombs hit one of our positions, killing one and wounding several other soldiers. Now our guns opened fire on the planes and shot one down. The pilot was a German. The entire squadron of P51s were flown by Germans. The planes had been some of ours that had been forced down and rebuilt by the Germans just for such a purpose. By making use of the autobahn as a runway and concealing the planes in the nearby forest, the Germans had developed combat airfields.

On another occasion our men were patrolling the

area near headquarters when a jeep with several American officers came up to our position. We had set up a road block and were screening all vehicles that passed by. Our men did not recognize the identification painted on the bumper of the jeep, so they stopped the vehicle and held the men at gun point. They sent for me, and I found our men talking with them about baseball. They seemed well informed, but one officer's accent seemed wrong to me, so I asked him where he came from in the States. He replied, "Philadelphia." I asked him if he wouldn't like to be back on La Salle Street. When he answered "yes !", I told our men to disarm the officers and take them to a nearby MP station. La Salle Street is in Chicago and not Philadelphia. I was right.

The officers were English-speaking Germans using captured American equipment and uniforms. When we had doubts about other vehicles and soldiers in the area, we had to check them very carefully. We did discover a few others trying to infiltrate our lines.

Before we crossed the Rhine River, the Battle of the Bulge was in full swing. Our battalion colonel set up headquarters in the town of Schulenheim in Alsace. My Battery, D, was closest to the front in that area. The day the Germans started to attack us, the colonel called all battery commanders and platoon leaders for a conference in Schulenheim, which was about twenty miles from our position. This left only two officers with us, but one had become very ill and had gone to the nearest field hospital. In the morning the other officer also was ill and had to go to the field hospital. Since our official first sergeant was away for one of his frequent medical treatments, it left me as acting first sergeant in charge of the battery. Our communications sergeant was in touch with the battery captain at headquarters by radio when

Art Goddard

shells began do drop around us. Headquarters ordered us to withdraw and proceed to the town of Schulenheim. They ordered me to lead the withdrawal. We had to go over snow covered hills and fields to reach Schulenheim. It was supposed to be a short cut route.

It was snowing hard that day. We noticed that the American flags that had been flying from most of the houses in the village were being replaced by swastikas and white flags. The civilians knew that the Germans were coming back. Part of our 10th Armored Division, which was between us and the Germans, was withdrawing also. The road that we were to travel on was cluttered with tanks and other vehicles. It was just about impossible to use. A French civilian who I had befriended offered some good advice.

He informed me that there was another partially paved road covered with snow that would be a quicker way to get to the town. He said he knew that the road was not mined and that it was seldom used. He agreed to go with us because he knew the road and stated that there were some very narrow places and a few bridges to cross. Although my French friend went with us, I sent a couple mine clearing engineers who were attached to us to go with the French friend ahead of the convoy. I followed them in a jeep and the rest of the battery followed me. We had hardly started when a tank accidentally hit one of our trucks, knocking it into a ditch. No one was hurt, and our men shoved the truck back onto the road and we continued. We reached Schulenheim ahead of the other batteries with no further difficulty. My French friend left us on the outskirts of the town. Later, because this action was well beyond my assigned duties, I received a commendation.

In Schulenheim the mayor of the town invited

me and a couple other men for dinner in his home. This turned out to be an interesting lesson about how Alsatians lived.

The mayor had been pro-French, and his wife was pro-German. The mayor spoke French, but his wife refused to speak anything except German. Two of their grown sons were present. One had been badly wounded while fighting on the Russian front and was on crutches. He had recently been discharged from the German army and sent home to recover. The other son was a member of the French underground who was there for a short visit. Although two of the family spoke French, and two spoke German, there was a local dialect that they all spoke. I had to switch from French to German and then to English for the sake of my buddies. It was very confusing and kept me too busy to eat much.

U.S. troops shoved the Germans back through the Maginot Line and then broke through the Siegfried Line in a few places. The Rhine River, however, was a major hurdle for the Allies to cross. The Germans withdrew to their side of the Rhine, blowing up most bridges across it. At Remagen the railroad bridge was still standing, and American troops rushed across it into Germany.

While in Alsace, the 431st was made a part of the 42nd Division, which was known as the Rainbow Division. We were no longer a separate battalion that could be shoved around from unit to unit as needed. We crossed the Rhine on a pontoon bridge near the German city of Worms. From there we followed the rapidly retreating Germans down an autobahn. For several miles we drove rapidly trying to catch up with them. The Germans pulled off the highway onto narrow roads leading into the forest that I believe was part of the Black Forest. As darkness closed in, our officers met to discuss strategy for the night. It was decided that we should take side roads that were shown on the map. These roads led into the forest, and we were to meet other units in a certain town.

We followed a narrow road that bordered a small river that flowed toward the main river near Wurzburg. It was agreed that we would stop for a few minutes each hour to make certain that the convoy stayed together. We had to drive close to the vehicle in front of us in order to see a reflector. No lights were allowed, and it was very dark with a little fog rising from the nearby river that we were following. I rode with the captain in his jeep and the jeep driver. We followed a regimental staff car of the 42nd Division and were followed by a two and a half ton truck.

At the first break our captain and the colonel in the regimental car in front of us agreed that the road we were on was not on our maps. They only knew that we were heading in the correct direction.

At the second break we were surprised to find the command car behind us and a different truck in front of us. We were unaware of any vehicle passing us. All drivers insisted that they had never lost sight of the reflector of the vehicle in front of them. It was very strange indeed! In a dark forest, vision was very difficult at night.

At the third break the regimental car was again in front of us and the original truck was behind us, but there were no other vehicles around. This was not only interesting, but very weird. It seemed as though the forest was closing in on us. I understood how so many tales had been written about the place. We had seen some short dirt roads leading off the one we were on, and we guessed that some vehicles had driven onto them.

At our fourth break we were completely alone, just the captain, the driver, and me. There was darkness all around us. We entered a small village, but did not find its name or any indication of a village on our map. I thought the village was the one where we were supposed to meet the rest of the battalion. The captain agreed with me and ordered our driver to pull into what appeared to be a fire station with its door opened. There was a large hook and ladder truck there. Our driver hid the jeep under the truck, and the three of us rolled out of the jeep onto the floor of the building and fell asleep.

The next morning as we awoke, we heard the sound of a truck and a familiar voice cry out to the driver, "Gazza, Do you see anyone? I don't know where we are!" It was our mess sergeant and our kitchen truck. At least we would eat.

This kitchen truck was the only other vehicle to reach that village that morning; it was the village designated for us to meet. We decided that we would wait there until the others arrived. By the end of the day nearly half of my battery had arrived, but it was three days before all the battalion got together.

My former gun crew had had an unusual experience. They had been following division vehicles during the night. They too checked each other hourly. The sergeant was puzzled when the vehicle he was following led him over a long pontoon bridge that crossed a wide river. His driver had lost sight of the reflector of the vehicle he was following, but he kept trying to catch up with it. The road followed a large river and as they rounded a curve, several American soldiers jumped in front of the truck to stop it. The sergeant reported that he was questioned about his I.D. and destination for nearly an hour. It was finally decided that his gun crew had been following a retreating German truck when it crossed the Main River. The men who stopped our truck had just crossed the river themselves and thought that only Germans were on that side of the river. They were fortunate in doing this before the bridge was destroyed by the Germans.

Finally our battery and the rest of the 431st Battalion were reorganized and ready to continue on to the city of Wurzburg. We fought our way through, village after village. German resistance was getting very weak. Sniper fire was our greatest threat as we entered the city of Wurzburg.

Wurzburg was divided by the Main River. The road reaching the Main from the southwest (our side) was between two hills. Our commanding officer ordered us to set up battery headquarters in a beautiful modern villa that overlooked the Main.

From a large picture window we could look out across a grassy bank that sloped down to the river. Across the river we were able to see German soldiers moving around in their tanks, trucks, and on foot. For some time no shots were fired by either side. Very heavy traffic blocked access to a bridge that our engineers were repairing. M.P.s were trying to organize traffic to move across the bridge, but there were so many soldiers, trucks, guns, jeeps, and all kinds of equipment, and no clear organization, that movement of the forces was almost impossible. Many were trying to cross at the same time. It was a very confused and disorganized area. Fortunately for us we were required to remain on our side of the Main in the beautiful villa, from which we could watch what was going on at the intersection as well as the streets on the other side of the river.

A major problem added to the confusion. There was a large warehouse at the entrance of the bridge that was full of liquor. Soldier after soldier entered the building as others came staggering out. I saw a colonel and a general enter the building to drive the men out. Our men transferred equipment from one truck to another so that a couple of the trucks were empty and now were filled with cases of liquor. I heard the general yell to the colonel, "These guys are all drunk!"

Fortunately the German troops had taken their share of the liquor also as they had crossed over the original bridge before blowing it up. The Germans were too drunk or confused to fire on us, but our men were too. It took the commanding general of the division to finally restore order out of the confusion.

Our anti-tank guns lined up on top of the hill behind our villa and began to fire over our heads at German tanks that were on the opposite side of the river. We saw some tanks hit, but the Germans did not return fire. Some of our men began to call the battle "The Drunken Battle of Wurzburg." I have never seen this description or name in any official account of the battle, however.

The men of one of our gun crews had crossed the bridge without their trucks or cannon. They found some German soldiers hiding in a railroad car on a railroad siding near the river. They disarmed the Germans, but soon they began to play cards and drink with them. They partied all night, and in the morning they allowed the Germans to leave, taking their guns and bottles with them. Some war this was!

The 42nd Division moved on through Germany, capturing towns and cities with little resistance. They took Nuremburg, which was later to be used for the war trials of the German leaders. My battery remained a few days in Furth, near Nuremberg, and then we pushed on to the Danube River. As we reached the Danube, German artillery began to shell us. There was a wooded area near the place where we were to cross the Danube. Some German shells exploded in the woods, and we were showered with shrapnel and wood fragments. Some of my buddies jumped into the river, but I climbed under a nearby tank. The river became bloody red as several of our men were hit, but I didn't think that I had been hit by the shelling. Several years after the war, little pieces of shrapnel worked their way out of my back. At first my family thought they were just "blackheads." A couple became infected and were removed surgically. It was metal. I am certain now that I got those pieces during that shelling. I never tried to claim this as an injury. Although the shelling lasted a long time, our artillery eventually silenced the Germans. We were able to continue on our way.

We had heard unbelievable stories about German concentration camps where Jews and anyone who disagreed with the Nazis were confined. As we approached the city of Munich we were close to the Dachau concentration camp. We joined with other units of the 42nd Division and others to enter the camp and liberate it. We had no idea what we would find in that camp.

SS Troops guarded the place and we had to take them down first. There was a train consisting of several cars, forty men and/or eight horses, on a siding near one of the buildings in the camp. There was a horrible smell coming from the building and also from the train. We slid the car doors open and found the car full of bodies. The bodies were too numerous to count. All were dead, and the floor was covered with feces and other horrible things. There was evidence of attempted cannibalism. One body near the door that I opened had its teeth imbedded in the shoulder of another. The nearby buildings had smoke pouring out of vents on the sides and roof and the smell of burning human flesh, which most of us couldn't tolerate. I had a small box camera and tried to take pictures, but I was too busy vomiting. One of my buddies did take pictures with my camera, however. Years later my wife thought those pictures were too horrible to keep, and she destroyed most of them.

We captured some SS guards who had been cruel to the prisoners. We freed scores of women prisoners who were still alive. Many of these women were Polish. Suddenly some of the women recognized an SS soldier whom I had just captured as one who had treated them inhumanly. The women attacked me to get that soldier. The only way I could have saved him was to fire into the mob of women, and this I could not do.

The women seized that SS guard and literally ripped him to pieces in front of me and my buddies. I still remember that sight, and it is very hard for me to write about it, but the truth must be told.

After the war it was reported by the Germans that although the Dachau Camp had crematoriums, they were never used. This was not true. There were furnaces burning, piles of ashes on the floor, bodies piled up awaiting cremation, etc. There were ditches dug outside the buildings full of bodies that had been thrown into them, but there had not been enough time for them to be covered up with dirt.

We captured or killed many SS troops there. We took those who were captured to a nearby prisoner of war camp. The prisoners whom we had freed were escorted to a displaced persons camp that was also close by. I tried to block out what I had seen, but I couldn't. I even drank a liter of rum and a liter of cognac, but this only made me very ill. I couldn't walk across the room, but I still remembered the horrors. I learned that alcohol just wasn't for me, and I have not drunk more than a sip or two of a dinner wine since. I can't even tolerate beer.

Art Goddard

A coke or a cup of coffee is enough for me.

Many years later in 1983, my wife and I visited Munich. I felt a compulsion to visit the Dachau Camp that was made into a park. My wife refused to go with me, and she stayed in Munich to do some shopping while I took a train to Dachau. Upon reaching the station in Dachau, I found that I would have a rather long walk to get to the camp. The expectation was bringing back so many memories that I decided to go no farther. I turned around and took the next train back to Munich where I joined my wife for some local sightseeing.

The night after we took Dachau, I was able to follow our battalion orders in spite of my drinking. I was required to type orders for our trucks to be emptied of all equipment and see that they were loaded with civilians from nearby communities.

We took the civilians to the camp, drove through it so that they could see the horrors that the Nazis had done, and then returned them to their community. There were some who already were saying that what went on in the concentration camps was simply Allied propaganda. We wanted the people to see for themselves. The civilians were horrified by the sights. Some cried; practically all became hysterical, and many fainted. All were confused and very upset, as we soldiers were. As for my buddies, they vowed never to fraternize with the Germans again; this vow lasted about two days.

The day after we took Dachau, some of the freed Polish prisoners had a party and invited three men from my battery who were of Polish ancestry and spoke the language. It became a huge drinking party and the liquor that some of them drank had been poisoned by the Germans. Many of the displaced people died, and of my three buddies, one died while drinking, another went blind, and the third said he never felt better in his life even though he drank from the same bottle as the others. That third buddy was drunk more than he was sober throughout the war, and I guess his system had become able to take the poisoned liquor. The one who went blind did eventually regain his sight several months after the War.

While we were near Munich we stayed at a beautiful resort on Lake Tagernsee. Shortly after we arrived, investigators from the U.S. Inspector General's office came to us and accused someone of stealing very valuable jewelry from a villa near our headquarters. They searched, but they found nothing. I had suspicions about one of my buddies, but I knew he was a successful gambler and frequently sent large amounts of money home to his family. After the war he wrote that he had saved enough to buy a business and also build a mansion for his family. Some of my other buddies shared similar suspicions about him, but so far as we knew, nothing was found to incriminate him. He died shortly after the war.

As the early days of May 1945 progressed, there were rumors that the war was ending in Europe. We learned that President Roosevelt had died shortly after returning from a war conference with Churchill and Stalin at Yalta in the Crimea of Russia. We learned that plans were made for dealing with Germany after the war, but it was to be our new President Truman who would carry them out. Another major conference of Allied leaders occurred at Potsdam, Germany.

The war was still going on against Japan. There was a possibility that we might be sent to the Pacific Theater now that most fighting in Europe was over.

Russian troops entered Berlin by April 1945. We heard that Hitler had finally married Eva Braun, and the two of them along with the Goebbels family had committed suicide in a bunker in Berlin. German soldiers had hastily dug shallow graves outside the bunker and placed Hitler and the others in them. They set the bodies on fire. When Russian troops took Berlin, they reported this, but there have been many conflicting stories about it. No matter what happened, World War II was over in Europe.

Shortly before he committed suicide, Hitler ordered Admiral Doenitz to replace him. Doenitz officially surrendered Germany to the Allies on May 7, 1945, and the following day, May 8, 1945, was recognized as V.E. Day– Victory in Europe Day. I was in the small Austrian town of Walchsee when I heard the news about V E Day!

The 431st Battalion was assigned to round up German soldiers in the Munich area. There was a "point system" that was a way to accumulate service points to determine who would be sent home and discharged from the army. As I remember, if we had 89 points, we would be eligible for discharge. One point was earned for each month of service, an extra point was granted for each month overseas, and each beach landing, battle area, decoration, etc. was worth five extra points. Almost all in my battalion had well over 100 points, hence the entire battalion was eligible to be discharged. I personally had almost 200 points. Our battalion was designated to remain as a unit that would soon return to the States. We could hardly wait!

We were sent to the German city of Bad Reichenhall near the Austrian border. We were assigned duties of screening civilians and other tasks performed by an army of occupation. Again, my ability to speak German as well as French and Italian kept me very busy interpreting. We took over a small hotel, the Mirabelle, which was owned by a doctor and used as an asthmatic clinic.

This city is close to Berchtesgaden, where Hitler had his "Eagle's Nest." High mountains surrounded the city that had not been badly damaged during the war. The railroad station and rail yards seemed to be the only parts of the city damaged.

Hitler had requested the people of Bad Reichenhall to allow him to build a retreat for himself on a mountain top overlooking the city, but the citizens refused him. This refusal was a good thing for the citizens of Bad Reichenhall because he punished the city by ordering his troops to ignore the city. The neighboring town of Berchtesgaden, however, cooperated, and Hitler built his retreat there.

As we entered the town, we drove up to the hotel where we were to make our headquarters. A lady came out and asked in perfect English what we wanted there.

When we told her that we were taking the hotel for our headquarters, she went inside and brought out a very dignified appearing lady who was introduced to us as the wife of the owner of the Mirabelle. The lady whom we first met was an American citizen who had been at the clinic when the war started, and she had been unable to leave. The family that owned the clinic allowed her to stay on, but later with their help she moved to an apartment of her own. She apparently was well-off financially. During the war, the doctor had become a high ranking officer in the medical department of the Volks Amy and was seldom present at the clinic.

The clinic that became our headquarters was also known as a hotel, and it offered luxuries for us. There was a huge dining room, and the owners arranged for their employees to serve us dinner each night. They also arranged for an orchestra from the community to play at dinner time. Our food was now a mixture of GI rations and German cooking. Most of my buddies enjoyed fraternization, but I was so busy interpreting, writing reports, etc., that I only visited the dining room a couple of times during the weeks we were there.

Some of our men had a weekend pass to visit Paris. Trucks took them from Bad Reichenhall to the railroad station in Strasbourg, where they transferred to a train that took them into Paris. It was a long trip, but the men had earned it. Since I had never had a furlough, I applied for one to visit my cousin Wally, whom I knew, was stationed in Chateau-Thierry, about 70 kilometers from Paris. I received the furlough and was told to go to Paris with the next weekend group and return with the following weekend group when they completed their three day pass to Paris. That gave me a full week furlough.

After the long and tiring trip to Paris, we were told we had to stay only in hotels operated by the American Red Cross and eat at Red Cross approved restaurants. I had no clearance with the Red Cross as I was expected to simply stay in Paris a few hours while waiting for the next train to Chateau Thierry. I could eat only at the transportation corps mess hall in the railroad station.

When I reached there, I left my buddies and went by local train to Chateau-Thierry. At the station there I discovered that my cousin was encamped nearly seven miles out of town. It was getting dark, but I started walking to his camp. There were other soldiers doing the same thing, and they knew it would be shorter if we cut across the World War I battlefield. It was nearly one o'clock in the morning when I reached his camp. I discovered that Wally had been transferred out that very day. His buddies at the camp put me up for the night, gave me a good breakfast the next morning, and drove me to the railroad station. It was a Sunday morning, and I found that the next train to Paris would not leave until Tuesday. I felt that I needed to join my buddies who were in Paris and return to our camp with them. I started to walk to Paris, but soon a GI truck came along and gave me a ride into the city. I found my buddies, who had another night they could spend in Paris before returning to camp.

A couple of my buddies persuaded me to stay in Paris until the next weekend when another group would come in from camp. I decided to stay if I could find a room somewhere. I took off most of my American ID from my uniform, and I looked like many of the French soldiers. In my best French I asked for a room in the Grande Hotel de Louvre and got one.

To my surprise the desk clerk himself showed me to the room. In the elevator he told me in perfect English that I didn't have to worry about speaking English there. He said there were many others in a similar situation already in the hotel.

The room was very large with twin beds and a sofa that could be converted into a bed. Four of us could stay there, so three of my buddies joined me for the one night. I had the room to myself for the rest of the week at a cost of only a couple dollars per day. It wouldn't be like that today.

I had a grand time exploring Paris. I visited the usual historical places and attended a show and a couple movies, but I had to eat all my meals at the transportation corps mess hall in the railroad station. I wanted to attend the Paris Opera, but they were sold out. While I was trying to obtain a ticket, I saw my battalion major and a couple other officers from my battalion. I knew that I was not supposed to be in Paris except for passing through the city, and I felt that they would consider me AWOL. I just knew that I would be in trouble when I got back to camp. I saw the French version of the musical "Rose Marie" that I had previously seen in London. I remember the French version better than the other. It was awfully risqué.

Upon returning to camp, I was called to the colonel's office. Expecting the worst, I was surprised when he said, "I hope you enjoyed Paris. Didn't you know that you had three days travel time on both sides of your furlough and you could have stayed another week?"

The colonel also informed me that he had recommended me for a commission in the State Department and that I was to return to Paris the next day for an interview at the U.S. Embassy.

I borrowed some money, returned to Paris where I stayed only one day, and filled out many papers. I was interviewed for more than an hour in French and was given a lecture about diplomacy. Most of the questions t I was asked dealt with my knowledge of French North Africa, and especially about the city of Dakar. After the interview I was sent back to my battalion.

Several days later I received orders from the War Department to report on October 30, 1945, to Boston, New Orleans, San Francisco, or Washington, D.C. for a written exam and induction into the State Department. I also received written orders to give to my commanding officer to provide necessary transportation for me to reach the closest location for that exam. I never went because I was discharged from the army on October 28, 1945. I was so busy celebrating my discharge that I completely forgot to report. A year later I received a letter from the State Department offering me another chance if I was still interested. I wasn't. I enjoyed teaching, and the city of Houston had become my home, so I declined.

Our battalion office work increased greatly during this time. In addition to interviewing civilians and displaced individuals, our battalion's size was greatly increased by the addition of soldiers from other units who were also ready for discharge.

I met several interesting people during the days I was at Bad Reichenhall. The daughter of the Nazi mayor of Munich was a frequent guest of the family who owned the Mirabelle. Although she seldom talked about her background, I discovered that one of her best friends had been Eva Braun. She apparently resented the way Hitler had treated her friend. Another buddy who also spoke German and I were frequent guests of the owner of the hotel in their apartment for lunch. The sister of the wife of the owner of the Mirabelle was often present at these luncheons. She seldom talked to us, but one day she told us her story.

Her husband had been a member of the Austrian cabinet, but he was not a Nazi. At the time of the Anschluss, he anticipated trouble for his family and had sent his wife to live with her sister in Bad Reichenhall. Her sister's husband, the doctor, had risen to high rank in the German people's army, so his wife would be safe there. His wife heard from her husband only three times after the Anschluss. He wrote that he was to be interviewed by the Gestapo the next day. His wife received a letter from the Gestapo stating that she could continue to live with her sister, but all their property had been taken by the Nazis, and her husband was being detained indefinitely. She was forbidden to return to Vienna.

A couple weeks later she received another letter from the Gestapo stating that her husband had died of natural causes and his body had been cremated.

In late September we left Bad Reichenhall for the French port of Le Havre to wait for our transport ship to return us to the States. We stayed a few days in Camp Lucky Strike until we could board the transport. While there I had another day's visit to Paris. Several members of my battery were also in Paris on a day pass, and some of them had become very intoxicated. Since I had the highest rank of those on pass, it was up to me to help anyone who got in trouble. I would have to deal with the French police as well as our own MPs. One of my buddies thought that he could do a better job directing traffic at the Place de La Concorde than the local police. He walked out into the middle of the street to direct the traffic. One of the first vehicles to come along was an American jeep with MPs in it. They arrested my buddy and carted him off to the military prison temporarily set up in the basement of the Paris Opera House. My other buddies found me, and accompanied by a couple of them who appeared sober, I managed to get him released to my custody. We got him to one of our trucks, and he slept there until we reached camp. I had finally got into the Paris Opera House, but not the way I wanted! The basement was indeed unpleasant, damp, and occupied by many prostitutes and other undesirables. It was a weird place, to say the least.

We sailed from Le Havre on a Liberty ship bound for Boston in the middle of October 1945. As we entered the port of Boston, we were greeted by fireboats shooting huge sprays of water into the air. Most ships in port blew their whistles and sirens as we wound our way up to a dock. There were trains waiting for us, and all we had to do was carry our baggage off the ship and take a few steps and board a train. We were home!

A train took us to Camp Miles Standish near Boston. From there we were sent to the post where we had been inducted. For me that was Fort Devens. I received back pay and a two week furlough. At the end of the two weeks I had to report back to Ft. Devens and receive my discharge papers. My grandmother lived just a few miles from the fort, so I hired a taxi to take me there. I was home!

Art Goddard

CHAPTER 7

HOME

After more than three and half years, I had arrived home, and I was ready to get on with the rest of my life. I was given a two week furlough upon arrival at Ft. Devens, in Massachusetts, and then returned for final discharge papers on October 28, 1945.

Ft. Devens was not far from my grandmother's house, so I hired a taxi to take me there. A couple of my buddies joined me, as they were heading for the railroad station in Fitchburg. We shared the cost of the taxi. The driver let me off at the foot of the short street where my grandmother lived. I knew that my grandfather and my aunt who lived there too were at work. A neighbor was probably staying with my grandmother, who was very ill with a bad heart condition. Grandmother had a watch dog that could be vicious if someone the dog did not know came close to the house. Grandmother could control the dog easily, but she was unable to get out of bed. As I approached the house, I saw the dog was loose outside.

He saw me and began barking and growling as he dashed toward me. I called out to him by name, and he stopped in his tracks and started waging his tail. Soon he was all over me with excitement. He remembered me; this made me feel welcome.

When I entered the house, Grandmother was alone. After a tearful welcome, she summoned her neighbor to meet me. She asked this neighbor to press my uniform, which was terribly wrinkled. Grandmother never liked messy clothes; she hadn't changed much.

After a few phone calls to other members of the family, my Aunt Bea came home from work.

She planned to ride with me by train to Williamstown in the late afternoon. We boarded the "Minute Man," the fastest train on the Boston and Maine Railroad. The train was overflowing with passengers, mostly soldiers heading for their homes. One soldier gave his seat to my aunt while I went to the dining car to get something to eat. I was very excited and restless. It took more than two hours for the train to reach my home town. When we arrived at the station, I found not only my parents, but also my aunt and uncle. These relatives were the parents of my cousin Wally whom I had visited in France. It was a joyful reunion.

During the two weeks I was home on furlough, my parents and I traveled over much of New England and New York visiting relatives and friends. I was under the shadow of having to report back to Ft. Devens to receive my final discharge papers. When I was given my papers, I started thinking seriously about finding a teaching position. I knew that I wanted to teach history in some high school, preferably near Boston. I applied for a job through a couple of teaching agencies and was soon called for an interview with the officials of the

Orange High School in Orange, Massachusetts. I took a job to start after the Christmas vacation. I was to teach Modern European History, Ancient History, and Latin II (Caesar), Latin III (Cicero), and Latin IV (Virgil). I had studied all these subjects, but I felt that I needed to brush up on them, especially the advanced Latin classes. I went to New York City, accompanied by a former high school friend, to look at available books to help me prepare. The time we were in New York City, we saw two stage shows and three movies in one day. My eyes were sore after that. I was thankful to get back home and rest up before starting my work in Orange.

When I accepted the position of teacher, I was told that it was only for one year because the Selective Service Act had provided that any one who was drafted could reclaim the position he had at the time. The school knew they were committed to reinstate many former teachers. Although I was entitled to return to Bridgeton Academy, I did not want to go back there. I wrote them a letter stating that I did not plan to return. This helped them a great deal, since they were having difficulty in placing those who had been drafted. I enjoyed my teaching in Orange, but I knew that there might not be an opening for me after that year. I would only teach there for the remainder of the school year.

Teaching at Orange was ideal for me at that time. The city was only thirty miles west of Fitchburg, where my grandmother lived, and sixty miles east of Williamstown. It was on the Boston and Maine Railroad, and I could easily go either direction. Since Grandmother was so ill, I went more frequently to her home on weekends than I did to Williamstown. I was able to help care for my grandmother.

I had received an offer to join the State Department. I was to report to take a written exam at the end of October, but I completely forgot. I never took the exam. When I was offered a second chance to take it, I did not want to do so. This determined that I would stay in education, and I have never regretted it.

Knowing that my stay in Orange was limited to one year, I applied to several schools in the general area around Boston for the following year. I was turned down by so many of the schools that I became very discouraged. One school superintendent told me that unless I was Italian or Irish and a Catholic, I wouldn't have a chance for a position in the greater Boston area.

I applied through an agency. that had arranged several interviews for me in other areas. One was with a Mrs. Margaret Kinkaid, who headed a private school in Houston, Texas. I enjoyed meeting her, but I did not want to go that far from home. My grandmother was dying, and the family was counting on my help over weekends. This interview with Mrs. Kinkaid was at the Christian Science Rest Home in Boston during June of 1946. Although Orange High School had ended its classes for the summer, they had a one time summer session, so I taught French and German. During that time, Grandmother died. Most of my family came to Fitchburg for the funeral.

Returning to Williamstown in August after the funeral, I still had no position for the coming year. I found several letters from my buddies, most of whom had gone back to work. There was one letter from Mrs. Kinkaid, asking me to reconsider her offer of a position to teach history in her upper school. On that same day, she called me to request another interview in Boston. I went back to Boston and, after a brief interview, I signed a contract to teach history at the Kinkaid School in Houston, Texas.

I had to change trains in St. Louis on the way to Houston. Since I had never been there, I decided to spend one night. While there, my father called me to say that there had been as many as eight offers from New England schools for me to teach starting immediately. Since I was under contract to teach in Houston, I turned down all the other offers. Today I feel that there must have been divine intervention, as I probably would have stayed in New England. I have been happy, and, I feel, successful with a full life in Houston.

William Kinkaid, Margaret Kinkaid's son, met me at the railroad station in Houston. His mother had arranged for me to have a room in a private home of a friend of hers. This home was within walking distance of the school. It was to cost me only $25.00 per month. Although my salary was a little more than what I made in Orange, there wasn't much money available. I was living on $1800.00 per year. I managed, however, and even saved enough to travel back to New England for Christmas and for summer vacations.

Shortly after returning home from the war, I had a couple personal things to straighten out. I had met a young lady in Maine before the war, and we wrote frequently about possibly sharing a life after the war. However, as the war came to an end, I felt that the chemistry was not right for us. I went to Portland for a day, and I found that she had found someone else. There was also a friend who grew up with me back in Williamstown, but she had started a very successful career as a nurse. I felt free to go to Houston. She remains a close family friend.

After settling into my room in Houston, William took me around the city and over to the school. I was favorably impressed by all that I saw. The school was a single floor, Spanish style building located on Richmond Avenue about five short blocks from where I had a room.

When I was interviewed by Mrs. Kinkaid, she told me that I would teach American History in her upper school. This was just what I had wanted. Because I had met Mrs. Kinkaid at the Christian Science Home in Boston, I feared that the school might be a religious school. She had assured me that it was non-denominational. I was very anxious to get started.

I arrived in Houston on the day before Labor Day. The next day, on Labor Day 1946, I went to the school and found several teachers passing out books and supplies to the students who came with their parents.

I met so many friendly people on that one day that I was overwhelmed. At the end of the day, Mrs. Kinkaid told me that she had liked the way I got along with the students of middle school age and their parents as well, so she thought that I should teach at the seventh and eighth grade levels. This suited me. I also realized that she wanted a man teacher for those grades. Later in the day, she said she had forgotten to tell me that the seventh grade history was Texas History. I told her that all I knew about Texas was what I had learned in American History classes. She said, "You'll be ready for it. You will come to dinner, and William and I will give you a crash course in Texas History." I went, they did, and I felt confident that I could teach it with their help.

When I first met Margaret Kinkaid in Boston, I was impressed by her enthusiasm for students, teaching, and education in general. She seemed to be a motherly type, but also a determined lady who knew what she wanted and how she would get it. I found some of the other teachers felt she was too domineering, but I was

Art Goddard

always comfortable in her presence. I discovered that she had spent many summers studying in colleges in various parts of the country. She did not want her school to be too insular. She wanted a diversified faculty. She was, however, very proud of her Texas background.

Mrs. Kinkaid ruled her school. There was a board of trustees helping her financially, but she was in charge! She was demanding of her faculty. She did not want them visiting with each other during school hours. There was no faculty lounge. She made it clear that she did not want any teacher to raise a voice to a child or touch them. She herself would step into the hallway, and, if she saw something she didn't like, with a clap of her hands, whatever was going on would come to an end.

I was aided by other teachers in getting started. Some of them were concerned about my social life. I was too busy and had too little money to think much about that. The Spanish teacher and her husband thought that I should see much of Texas, and they frequently took me to places on weekends such as Galveston, Kemah, and the San Jacinto monument. I was interested in learning more about the state, and on an occasional weekend I would go by bus to San Antonio, Dallas, or Austin, just to get acquainted with the state. I had no car. When I arrived in Houston, I knew only two people in the entire state of Texas. Mrs. Kinkaid was one, and my battery medic during World War II was the other. He lived near a little village called Sweet Home. He invited me to spend a weekend a couple times, but I was too busy most of the time.

I started to teach at Kinkaid in September 1946, and I was able to save enough money to purchase a round trip ticket back to Williamstown for the Christmas Holidays. For several years following this I made two trips per year back to New England for Christmas and summer vacations. I had decided that I would vary the routes I would take. In those days several railroads were available, providing different routes. I had a chance to visit New Orleans, Chicago, Washington, New York, and other places as I arranged to spend a night in each place between train connections. My favorite turned out to be the Santa Fe Railroad from Houston to Chicago, and then on the New York Central from Chicago to Albany, New York. My parents or a friend met me in Albany, which was only forty miles from Williamstown. I really got to know the railroads. I enjoyed traveling by rail very much!

Mrs. Kinkaid demanded a lot from her teachers. She informed me that I was expected to be at school on duty daily from seven in the morning until five in the afternoon. There was no real lunch break.

Students ate outdoors or in a shed that was called "The Shelter House" It was a covered walkway rather than a shed. Most students brought a bag of sandwiches for lunch. Or, they would buy soup or something hot from a caterer, whose name was Andrew, in the shelter house.

My schedule during my first year at Kinkaid was to teach all eighth grade history, seventh grade history, and one section of Ancient History at the ninth grade level. In those days there were two graduations per year–one in January and the other in June. This meant that there was what we called high level for those promoted in January and low level for those promoted in June. I was also on duty at lunch times, and there was a study hall that was supervised on a rotating basis. Since I had no way to prepare sandwiches in my room, I usually was given one by another teacher or by a student.

My students were of great help to me in those early days of teaching, especially those in my seventh grade Texas History classes. The students realized that a Yankee teaching Texas History probably didn't know much about the state. Several of those students and their parents decided to teach me more about Texas than was in the text book. I was a willing learner. Even today, some fifty years later, one or another of those students look me up and we have great discussions about how they taught me.

One of the routines of the school was for teachers to submit reports each Friday to Mrs. Kinkaid.

We had forms to fill out involving academic progress for our classes, special forms for certain individuals, a report on any telephone or personal discussion with a parent, and a request sheet for supplies ranging from paper clips to writing paper. The school was very well organized. It was obvious that Mrs. Kinkaid wanted to know about everything that went on.

One of the teachers told me that Jerome, a janitor, would trim bushes outside open classroom windows and would report what was going on in the classroom to Mrs. Kinkaid. This was one of the ways she checked on students and classrooms. I also discovered that occasionally when there had been mischievousness in the boys' bathroom, she would have a janitor in the attic who could peer down through a small window and check on what went on.

Shortly after I started teaching, another one of the new teachers and I revolted over part of the reporting system. We were expected to turn in reports in triplicate, so this teacher and I used carbon paper to make copies. When we turned these reports in, Mrs. Kinkaid sent them back to us to do them again in handwriting. She did not accept carbon copies. We had to do them before leaving the school. After this, my reports were always on time on Friday.

Mrs. Kinkaid enjoyed music. Twice each week there was an assembly period in the study hall for a sing-a-long. The classes met in the study hall for this. I became very much involved with this because I could sing. In addition, each day started with a short chapel program. Mrs. Kinkaid provided responsive readings that we used. I discovered that there were certain hymns and songs, such as "Onward Christian Soldiers," which she disapproved of and asked me not to use. Reluctantly I abided by her wishes.

At the graduation ceremony each year, there was a pageant involving the entire school from kindergarten up. Such programs required considerable rehearsal time, and during the late spring, time was taken out of the afternoon curriculum for such rehearsals. This pageant was just one tradition that Mrs. Kinkaid gave the school. A couple times these pageants at graduation created unusual circumstances.

One graduation day it rained very hard. Never before had a graduation been postponed because of rain, and that day was no exception. The graduation ceremonies were in the yard behind the school. We usually rented an organ and hired an organist to play for the ceremony. Our school music teacher directed the pageants with the aid of several teachers, including me. That day when it rained so hard all morning, the faculty and many parents thought the graduation ceremony should be postponed. But Mrs. Kinkaid insisted that it would clear in time for the pageant. It did. Janitors and some teachers and parents dried off the chairs that had been set up for the parents, the organ, piano, and the platforms used in

Art Goddard

the ceremony. The pageant went off very well, but less than a half hour after it was over, it started to rain hard again. Mrs. Kinkaid had told everyone to pray for no rain. The fact that the rain stopped led people to say that Mrs. Kinkaid must have a "pipeline" to God.

At the end of my first year at Kinkaid, the eighth grade English teacher, who had acted as head of that part of the school, decided to resign and accept a position in the Houston public schools. This teacher had made schedules for faculty and students, discussed problems with students, their parents, etc. There was no Principal or even a division separating students of the middle grades from the rest. There was a Principal of The Lower School, Marie Keeler, who handled problems through the fifth grade.

She was a wonderful school lady and very helpful to all teachers. William Kinkaid was Principal of The Upper School. The eighth grade English teacher more or less presided over the middle grades.

When the eighth grade English teacher left, the seventh grade English teacher was next in line to make schedules and control the area. She was a wonderful teacher and a very kind lady, but she had trouble making boys behave. One day during an assembly the boys were acting up badly, even calling her bad names. I had been a first sergeant in the army, and I couldn't stand for the way the boys were treating her. I raised my voice like a First Sergeant, everyone quieted down, and then I lectured them about respect to an adult and authority. I did not know that Mrs. Kinkaid was in the hallway and heard me raise my voice. Other teachers reminded me that she had made it clear that anyone who shouted at the students or laid a hand on them would be fired. The other teachers told me that I wouldn't be around the next day because of what I did. Sure enough, I received a note from the office to report to Mrs. Kinkaid at the close of school.

When I entered Mrs. Kinkaid's office, I expected to be fired. She reminded me that she did not approve of teachers raising their voices, but she also said that those students deserved it. She then said that effective the next day, grades six, seven, and eight would be known as Kinkaid's Middle School. She added that I was their first Principal and would continue teaching history at those levels. She said she would raise my salary by ten dollars each month. This was very pleasant.

Shortly after I became Principal, I had to deal with a difficult problem created by one of our teachers. This teacher was an excellent teacher who had very high standards for his students.

During the mid-year exam period, he became disturbed by the poor penmanship some of his students had. He took their exams from them, tore them up, told them he was failing them, and then brought the fragments to me. The time for the exam had just ended, and tearful students staggered into my classroom. They didn't know what to do, and they were afraid that he would fail them all.

I took the fragments to Mrs. Kinkaid, showing her what the teacher had done and why. She told me to collect all the papers and sit in her office while she sent for that teacher. She also sent for her son. She scolded the teacher and told me to make certain that he patched the papers together and really graded them. She asked me to spot grade some of the papers after the teacher was finished. Bill Kinkaid was very angry at the teacher. For a few minutes I thought he was going to fight him, but Mrs. Kinkaid got between them and everyone settled down. The teacher did a good job of patching and grading, and the students did quite well on the exam after all. This introduced me to the kind of problems that I might face as principal. That teacher finished the school year, but he was not asked to return.

One of the teachers introduced me to the Pastor of the First Presbyterian Church. He invited me to attend a choir rehearsal at his church. I told him that I would visit one rehearsal, but that I wasn't sure I wanted to get involved with a choir. World War II had indirectly destroyed my interest in singing. Also, I found that I had lost much of my natural ability. He encouraged me to go back to a choir believing that I would regain some of my volume and interest.

One of the choir members was related to Nelson Eddy, a famous actor and movie singer of those days.

Some people had developed the habit of going to his home for dinner and a music listening session after church services on Sundays. There were about a dozen of us, and some friends from other churches joined us after dinner. The group was about equal between men and women. We began to travel around together. I remember going to the Metropolitan Opera to see the opera "Aida" when it performed in Houston. My seat was in the old auditorium on concrete steps in the back of the building. It was very hot and without air conditioning. The lady playing the part of Aida became ill during the first act and had to be replaced. It was a very uncomfortable experience, which is probably why I remember it so well. The auditorium was very dirty; there had been a wrestling match there the previous evening. In those days in Houston, there were very few theaters other than movie houses. I went with this group of friends to Dallas once to see another opera in a much better building.

When I started teaching, I knew that I did not have a teaching certificate for teaching in Texas. Mrs. Kinkaid insisted that such a certificate was not necessary for teaching in a private school, but I wanted to do things correctly. I went back to college during summer until I completed the correct courses for certification. I already had a master's degree in education, but I had no college credits in English. For three summers in a row I went to Boston University, fulfilling the necessary English requirements as well as other educational courses that I felt would be helpful in my work in Houston. I found that all I needed to obtain a Doctorate in Education were three more course credit hours, plus a thesis. I talked it over with Mrs. Kinkaid, who convinced me that I already had enough college credits except for one in Texas History and Government, which I could obtain at the University of Houston.

Since I was already teaching Texas History, I found the course easy. For the final exam, the professor handed out the usual blue books for essay type tests. He wrote five questions on the blackboard and instructed the class to write on any four during the two-hour period allowed. I found the questions to be very easy. After twenty minutes the professor announced that he had forgotten that he had to make a speech in Galveston. He asked us to stop writing and he would only grade us on what we had done.

I was confident that I should receive an A. I didn't receive any notice of a grade from the university, and I was so busy at school that I forgot about the course for several weeks. When I remembered that I had not received a grade, I called the university. They indicated that the professor hadn't sent in a grade for me because I only audited the course. I convinced the university

Art Goddard

that I had taken the course for credit and had paid the required fee. A few weeks later I received a letter from the university stating that the professor had died without leaving any record of my performance. I was informed that I could take a special exam for advanced standing in the course, and that would give me the credit I needed. I went back to the university the following Saturday and took that exam, which was far more difficult than the other one had been. It consisted of 500 objective type questions. I was pleased when I received a grade of 89.

Not only had I joined the choir of the First Presbyterian Church, but the Kinkaid music teacher involved me with a few singing sessions at her home. She usually had several members of her church choir in attendance, and she pressured me to join her choir. I sang under her direction at the St. Stephens Episcopal Church for several months. Each summer I went back to New England, and when I returned to Houston, I started singing in a different church.

I sang one year with the First Methodist Church. All this time, I still went around with the group who listened to classical music on Sunday afternoons. One member of this group, Kermit Lewis, had become one of my best friends, and we double dated frequently. He decided to join the First Methodist Church and persuaded me to do the same.

It was at the First Methodist Church in 1951 that I first met a young lady named Ruth Wilke. It didn't take long before I decided that I wanted her to be my wife.

The year 1951 was a very significant one in my life. Not only had I found the girl I wanted, but great changes were going on at school. Mrs. Kinkaid and her son William had decided to retire. There was a search for a new head of the school. After interviewing a few, the committee and Mrs. Kinkaid agreed to hire John Hancock Cooper as headmaster. Along with John Cooper, the school hired Carl Reed to be Principal of the Upper School. Carl's wife, Sonny Reed, was hired to be a study hall teacher in my department and also to do some clerical work for me. This was the first time that I had any administrative help.

Another development occurred in 1951. The school's music teacher, who was also the choir director at St. Stephens Church where I was singing, loved Gilbert and Sullivan Operas, as I did. She had performed in several operas and operettas in New York before coming to Houston. Those of us who met at her house frequently for singing sessions began to sing Gilbert and Sullivan shows seriously. Eleanor Miller obtained several copies of "H.M.S.Pinafore," which we enjoyed singing. When John Cooper, the new headmaster of Kinkaid, heard about our group, he joined us. He had sung frequently in Gilbert and Sullivan shows in the Northeast.

He felt that those shows could also be done by high school music departments, and he encouraged our music department to do one each spring for the next several years.

In the summer of 1951, the singing group with Mrs. Miller felt we should do some kind of a performance of "H.M.S. Pinafore." John Cooper arranged for us to have the little gym at Kinkaid, and we did perform it. We did it without costumes and we used our music scores.

I shared the part of "Ralph "with a tenor, Bill Robinson, who also sang in the St. Stephens Choir. We identified our parts by wearing a sign. We did this in front of a small audience of friends and colleagues, but we felt that we should go further.

Houston lacked in good summer entertainment,

and we planned to do a performance in 1952 of Gilbert and Sullivan's "The Gondoliers." Thanks to John Cooper, arrangements were made to perform at the Cullen Auditorium at the University of Houston. The head of the Music Department of the University of Houston enjoyed Gilbert and Sullivan operas and agreed to be our director. We also decided that we should obtain a charter from the state and organize as a performing organization. We obtained the charter, elected some officers and were recognized as a performing group. Although I was involved with chartering the group, I did not sing in its first production. My thoughts were heading toward marrying Ruth Wilke. I went back to New England again in July and August and arranged for financing a new car upon returning to Houston. In October, I asked Ruth to marry me and was delighted when she agreed.

On December 20, 1952, Ruth and I were married by Reverend Brown in the chapel of the First Methodist Church. We wanted it to be a small and intimate wedding.

My parents came down from Massachusetts, and Ruth's father, her sister and brother-in-law attended. Ruth's mother was ill that day, and her brother was somewhere in Korea at the time. Ruth's sister Dolly was her Maid of Honor, and Kermit Lewis was my Best Man. We had not announced the wedding at our work, but a few teachers and some of Ruth's colleagues found out and attended. Two of my former students were there also. Both of those students had worked well with me, and we had developed excellent student-teacher relationships.

Ruth's sister Dolly had a reception for us in her home after the wedding. Ruth and I drove to New Orleans for our honeymoon. We planned to stay only a few days as we wanted to be back in Houston in time for Christmas. We enjoyed New Orleans very much and have returned there occasionally since.

We decided to live briefly in my apartment on Graustark Street, but neither of us liked it. Ruth worked at Great Southern Life Insurance, and I was teaching at Kinkaid. Both places of employment were on Richmond Rd. . The apartment was within easy walking distance, but we decided to move. We bought a house at 9615 Belneath Street in the east part of Houston. That area was growing rapidly, and we moved there in 1954. We had several parties at our home for teachers, Ruth's colleagues, members of the Gilbert and Sullivan Opera Company, and our many friends. Soon other events occurred that made us think of moving again.

The new head of Kinkaid realized that I needed a new study hall teacher who could help me with some administrative duties. Carl and Sonny Reed had decided to move on to another school in Florida. John Cooper felt that he needed an administrative assistant who could work well with parents.

John had a very talented and hard working teacher at his previous school, Leigh Weld, so he persuaded Leigh and his wife Velma to come to Houston and work at Kinkaid. Leigh would teach math at the fifth grade level (later sixth grade) and help me with sixth grade responsibilities. He would also be John's administrative assistant. Later he was also Assistant Principal of the Middle School. He gave me much needed, valuable support. Velma Weld had been a nurse, and until then Kinkaid had no nurse.

Velma became my study hall teacher, assisted me with clerical work, and served as school nurse. When we became involved with the interim term travel programs, both Leigh and Velma were outstanding help to me.

Art Goddard

On October 14, 1956, our son David Wilke Goddard was born at Hermann Hospital in Houston. The day David was born, Ruth's brother, Ted Wilke, discharged home from the navy, stayed with us most of the time while we waited for David's birth. In fact, we waited from about 2:00 P.M. on the 13th to 7:00 A.M. on the 14th for him. Ted teased me often through the years, saying that I, who didn't smoke, actually smoked most of his package of cigarettes that night. I still don't remember doing that, and I know I haven't smoked since. David's birth was an exciting time!

In 1957, Kinkaid School moved from the Richmond Ave. location to a new area off Memorial Drive. The school was built there on 48 acres of land. It was not easy for me to drive from Belneath St. to the school, and besides, with the arrival of David we wanted a three bedroom house. The Belneath house had only two small bedrooms. We began to look for another house. One of the teachers at Kinkaid had moved into a new house in an area called Campbell Woods that was part of the Spring Branch section of Houston. We found a house there and moved into it in January 1957.

In the fall of 1957, Kinkaid School moved into its new buildings on Kinkaid School Drive near the intersection of Memorial Drive and San Felipe St.

The new school gave me considerably more room. Classrooms were on a U-shaped hallway and were joined to the upper school by a study hall room and shared library. My office was like a glass cage near one of the entrances to the school. It was easy for me to monitor the hallways All this occurred before the Reeds had decided to leave Kinkaid. Sonny Reed ran the study hall and assisted me with paper work in the office. I continued to teach all eighth graders' U.S.History. The classes were very large. The school required Latin at the eighth grade level. To help the Latin teachers by keeping their class size down, I usually taught one or two sections. Plans were made for a new library that would serve both the upper and middle schools. Thanks to the Moran family, a new library was built that also contained a large lecture room for me to use for my classes.

In 1958 my parents moved from Williamstown to Houston. They stayed with us for a few weeks. In December 1959 my father had a stroke. Our family doctor arranged for him to be treated by Dr. De Bakey's group in the Methodist Hospital. They found that he needed heart by-pass surgery. He survived the surgery but had another major stroke; he never regained consciousness. He is buried in Memorial Oaks Cemetery where Ruth and I had purchased burial spaces a few years before.

After my father died, my mother returned to Massachusetts, planning to live with her sister Pearl in North Adams. While she was in North Adams, John Cooper offered her a position as a receptionist at Kinkaid. She accepted, and I flew to New England to drive her back to Houston. Soon she found an apartment near us where she lived for more than thirty years. Mother worked for the school for over ten years before she retired.

My summer routine had changed after my marriage. Ruth and I went to New England a few times after David was born, and we always took David with us on our trips. Each summer during the sixties and seventies we went on a vacation. Ruth had gone back to work when David entered school, and David attended Kinkaid up through the fourth grade. We felt that it was increasingly difficult for him because his dad was a Principal there.

He entered the Spring Branch Schools and graduated in the first graduating class of Northbrook High

Art Goddard

School. After graduation, David attended Sam Houston State University and received B.A. degree in Radio/TV/Film, with a minor in Music. He has worked for over 25 years as a D.J. and has been with KSBJ for at least 20 years on a part time basis. Each Sunday morning he gets up at 3:30am and is on the way to KSBJ by 3:45am.

For the 50th anniversary performance of The Houston Gilbert and Sullivan Society's performance of "The Pirates of Penzance," David helped produce a CD. I think he has archived about 20 years of performances in recordings.

Ruth left Great Southern Life Insurance to work first in stores, and then in banks. After 17 years with what became Wells Fargo Bank, she retired in 1994. I kept on with my school work. Education means so much to me.

I found that John Cooper was an excellent person to work with. He and I both realized that many ideas were being tried out in other schools, and we felt that we should investigate them to determine if we wanted to try any of them at Kinkaid. He sent me to visit schools in New Orleans, St. Louis, and New York City to see what they were doing at the middle school levels.

I found that we were really ahead of most of the schools already. John and I insisted that the major hidden curriculum for middle school courses was to continue to develop better study skills. I promoted a special technique in my history classes that I called S.Q.3R. These stood for survey or scan a reading assignment, question yourself what it was about and why did one have to know it, read it rapidly for the over all picture, then read it again slowly, taking notes this time.

These notes should be based on answers to questions "who, what, when, where, why, and how." From the notes, one could drill for mastering details and understanding significance.

This study skill procedure became so popular that John had me teach sessions in study skills on Saturdays to any students, teachers, or parents who wished to attend. My Saturdays soon became very busy with these sessions, which overflowed from the study hall into the hallways. I had been told by several students who had been asked to outline in other subjects that they didn't know how to find what to put into such an outline. These concerns caused me to enlarge and adapt this study procedure that I found had been used in the early twentieth century at other schools. Although I used it at the eighth grade level, the sixth grade history teacher still uses it at her level. This teacher, Barbara Cooney, was hired in the seventies to assist me and she learned the procedure then.

During the sixties and seventies I was asked to be on committees to evaluate other schools, especially their middle schools. I also represented the School at ERB meetings and conventions. I administered college board exams at Kinkaid, and I attended conventions of independent schools both of the Southwest and also national. I was a member of the National History Society and attended many of their conventions.

All of this kept me very busy during the school year. During summer vacation time, I had to plan the next year's work for the entire middle school, make faculty and student schedules, and hold conferences with parents and others. As head of the middle school, I was also involved with testing and interviewing new students for the school. We had a summer school also, and I taught English there for six weeks. Although the headmaster was in charge of the summer school, he asked me to make schedules and decide on faculty.

Kinkaid, like most other Texas schools, dropped the mid-year graduation programs. Summer school gave students a chance to decide whether they wanted to advance a semester or remain in lower sections.

During summer school times, I usually taught eighth grade English. I enjoyed the opportunity to encourage creative writing. I would give the class a few sentences of a story and stop at an interesting place and ask the students to finish the story. Occasionally one of the pupils of those days reminds me today about that technique.

My summers also involved singing in Gilbert and Sullivan Operettas. We usually started rehearsing in June and held performances in late July. As soon as the last performance for the season was over, Ruth, David, and I would leave on a two weeks vacation before returning just in time to start the new school year. I served as President of the Gilbert and Sullivan Society a couple of times. I was President of it when the society moved its performances from the Cullen Auditorium, in the University of Houston, to the new downtown Jones Hall. For several years I was also Treasurer of the Society. On the day of the final performance, I would set up an office in the bedroom of one of my former students at Kinkaid, Charles Sanders, who also sang in the Gilbert and Sullivan chorus. There I would count the money, pay the bills, and prepare reports while the rest of the cast was partying. Charles helped me a great deal, and I am happy to say that today he is still one of my best friends.

During the 1970s Kinkaid, like many other schools throughout the country, experimented with various ideas in education. Kinkaid tried the open classroom procedure. Because of the social nature of middle school students, I objected to it at that level. It seemed to be successful in our lower school for several years, but today walls are up.

During the sixties and early seventies, we tried an "Interim Term" in both The Middle School and Upper School. This was a time when teachers could, for a short time, present other subject matter other than the required curriculum. It didn't work out well in my department, but it was very successful in our Upper School.

One day John Cooper and I were discussing possible ways to enhance class identities. John suggested a musical contest between the grades. We decided to try this and planned a short rehearsal time for each grade, replacing other activities for a few days. This would be followed by an assembly. We called the program the "Little Brown Jug" contest. Each class would prepare a folk song, a round, a patriotic song, a popular song, and a specialty number. We decided that teachers who were not music or drama teachers would lead these contests. They became very popular and something of a tradition for the school. Today the program is presented by grades five and six, while seventh and eighth graders are gone on historical educational tours.

John and I planned a special week instead of the "Interim Term" for the middle school. At the sixth grade level, the students would spend several days at a ranch.

The seventh grade, because Texas History was part of the curriculum, would tour Austin, San Antonio, and other important Texas cites. Since U.S. History was taught in the 8th grade, that grade would fly to the Northeast and spend days in Washington, Philadelphia, Gettysburg, Williamsburg, Annapolis, and occasionally Boston.

In the 1970s I was becoming increasingly tired and knew that I had to slow down.

During the summer of 1972, we planned to take a leisurely driving trip to the Pacific Northwest. I had just purchased a new car. On the day of the final Gilbert and Sullivan performance of "The Gondoliers," we left as soon as we could after I got home after the show.

Rising at 4:00 A.M. we started out. Ruth and I shared the driving, and we drove to Lubbock, Texas that first day. I realized that I had some kind of a stomach upset, but we got up early the next morning and drove to Durango, Colorado. We checked into a motel and went for dinner. I felt very strange and told Ruth that I might be having a heart attack. She drove me to a local hospital. The doctors stabilized me and kept me for four days. I was suffering from fatigue. When I left the hospital, we drove back to Houston where our family doctor persuaded me to slow down.

I decided to stop singing in Gilbert and Sullivan shows each summer. This was a hard decision because I had enjoyed doing them for twenty-one years. I did remain on the Society's board for several more years. The school decided to give me more help in both administration and teaching, hiring a young man out of college who would team teach with me and also assist in athletics. He latter became head of our athletic department.

I held counseling sessions with each eighth grader and parents individually during the late winter sessions. During that time, the assistant teacher did most of the teaching. However, I still gave lectures, prepared exams, and gave the grades for the students. I often was involved with the search and hiring of new faculty members. One of those was John Germann, who today is head of the History Department of the school. He and his wife Caro Ann have a little country weekend place neighboring ours, about fifty miles west of Houston. They are among our best friends.

Our first "Know your State" trip to the San Antonio area was in 1971; I organized and led this tour that I enjoyed very much. It went over so well with the students, their parents, and the school in general that it became part of the school year for 7th graders. Because of the success of the seventh grade trip, we took 8th graders to Gettysburg, Philadelphia, Williamsburg, and Washington. This too was very successful.

In 1972 I went on both the seventh and eighth grade trips, but it was too much. After that I went only on eighth grade trips until I retired. During the final 10 trips, our son David went along as a chaperon and to watch over me. He loved it, and I enjoyed having him with me. It made it a lot of fun for me. These trips were in February in spite of the cold weather in the North. It was a "dead week" in our sports programs, hence easy for students to have time off and for me to use coaches as chaperones.

These trips required a great deal of advance preparation. I arranged with a travel agency to handle the first Washington trip, but after that I served as my own travel agent. On our third trip we had a problem that made me realize that I should go up the day before the class, in order to make certain proper room arrangements were made. We had sent rooming lists to the Sheraton Park Hotel in Washington where we were to stay. A clerk there had taken our lists, without attention to boy or girl or chaperon, rearranged it in alphabetical order, and handed out room keys in that order when we arrived.

The result was great confusion when we checked about 9:00 P.M. With the aid of one of my very capable chaperones, Elisabeth Beck, we spent hours working with hotel management to redo the lists. It was after midnight when all were comfortable in a room. After that experience I always went ahead of the students to check lists, obtain room keys, and hand them out when the group arrived.

These Washington trips were also a lot of fun for us all. In 1979 we arrived by two planes in the midst of a very heavy snow storm on a Saturday. The next morning there was so much snow on the ground that all transportation was canceled.

The hotel personnel were concerned about us because we couldn't get out, but our students came to the rescue. The girls set up a buffet of sorts in one of their rooms with food they had smuggled in with their luggage. The boys planned entertainment for our dinner time. One of our bus drivers had plowed through the snow with his little car, and he and two of the chaperons drove around until they finally found a small convenience store where they bought more food. The students had a snow sculpture contest that occupied most of the day. The next morning transportation was still canceled, but our bus drivers checked out their buses before their garage was closed for the day because of the storm. We went by buses, following snow plows that were clearing the roads, all the way to Williamsburg, Virginia. The streets in Williamsburg were cleared. By the time we were ready to return to Washington, most roads were clear, and we had no further difficulty.

Each of these trips with eighth graders was an adventure. Let me write about the one that caused me the greatest concern. We checked into the Sheraton Park Hotel in Washington, this time with no difficulty.

The boys were assigned rooms on the second floor and the girls on the floor above them. These rooms overlooked the main entrance to the hotel. We were told that

Vice President Agnew at that time lived in a suite in the hotel. Because of his presence, we arranged with local police for a special canine patrol to watch the hallways at night.

Late that night I was meeting with other chaperones, planning some changes in our schedule for the next day when police, hotel management, secret service, and others arrived with drawn guns. I opened my door and was terrified when I saw them. They wanted to know who was in charge of the group. After I identified myself and others and explained that we were a school group, the police informed me that some boys from one of our rooms had opened the window and were throwing ice cubes up to the girls' room above them. The ice cubes had dropped down on a taxi in the driveway below. The driver thought he was being shot at and turned in a security alarm. After a stormy night with the boys and phone calls back to the school about it, I decided to send the boys who had caused the problem back to Houston on the next available flight. They had broken several rules we had set for their behavior. Back in Houston, we were praised for the way we handled the situation. Because of our action, we almost never had trouble with students on these trips.

I led the Washington area trips for twenty-one years, until I retired. I found them to be a good change of pace not only for students, but also for the teachers and possibly their parents.

Ruth, David and I continued to take summer vacation trips. Many of them were to visit my relatives in New England or Florida. Occasionally my Aunt Bea would visit us in Houston.

In 1971 my aunt and a lady friend of hers were arriving to spend Christmas with us. On Christmas Eve,

David and I were planning to go to the airport to meet them while Ruth was working. David and I decided to go to the local health spa before going to the airport. When we returned home from the spa, we were startled to see fire trucks at our house. A short circuit had occurred in an electric clock in our kitchen. This clock had been making funny grinding noises for some time. It burned the wall, damaging the kitchen and the adjoining hall. There was heavy smoke damage throughout the house. We had to move out, and we rented an apartment for three months until the damage was repaired. That year we had Christmas in my mother's small apartment. There has never been another electric wall clock in our house.

In the 1950s I lost my father; in the 1960s Ruth lost her sister, Dolly, and her father; and in the 1970's Ruth lost her mother and her brother-in-law. In 1981, David graduated from Sam Houston University and lived with us, while working. My mother continued to work as receptionist at Kinkaid, and Ruth and I continued to work. In 1983 the school offered me some financial help for me to take a European trip back to places where I had been during World War II. In July Ruth and I flew to Amsterdam. We toured the Netherlands, Germany, Switzerland, Belgium, France and England. Two days before the trip, Ruth injured her knee. The doctor provided her with a soft cast so that she could go on the trip, and she very bravely walked all over the places we went usually on crutches. It was very painful for her, but she stayed with it.

In 1984, I decided it was time for me to lighten my school load even more. John Cooper had retired as headmaster in 1979, and Glenn Ballard had become our new headmaster.

He suggested that I might find someone whom I

could recommend as principal, but he said that I could stay on as a teacher. We had had a visiting teacher from Philadelphia who I respected greatly. He was Joseph Ludwig, who at the time was head of the middle school of Friends Central School in Philadelphia. In 1984 he agreed to move to Houston and head our middle school. He wanted me to stay on as a teacher and to run the Washington trips. This arrangement was more than satisfactory. Joe and his family became very close friends, not only for Ruth and me but also for David and my mother.

Joe discovered that his old school in Philadelphia was expanding with a new lower school at a different site. He was asked to return there as principal of their lower school and also to serve as assistant headmaster of the entire school. After three years with us, Joe and his family returned to Philadelphia. We are still good friends.

Kinkaid needed time to search for another principal. I volunteered to go back for one year as an Interim Principal, thus giving the school time to find a new one. In 1988 John Thomas became principal of Kinkaid Middle School. He was a wonderful choice. He was very well received by all, and stayed with us for four years. When John Thomas left, Bob Beck, a very able teacher and administrator who had worked with me before, followed John Thomas as an interim principal of the middle school. Following Bob, Mark Devey was Principal for three years, and then John Friday. John taught Latin in our upper school for several years, and he knew the school well. John was very well qualified and well liked by all.

In 1988, after John Thomas became Principal of The Middle School, I took my retirement at the age of seventy, but I was not through at the school. Glenn Ballard asked me to evaluate faculty from pre-K through The Upper School on a part time basis.

I made my own schedule and followed my own procedure for this. I evaluated faculty from 1989 to 1996. I started at Kinkaid in 1946. From 1946 to 1984, I taught and was also Principal of The Middle School. From 1984 to 1987, I continued teaching while Joe Ludwig was Principal. From 1987 to 1988, I taught and was Principal again. From 1988 to 1996, I evaluated faculty. In all I had worked at Kinkaid School for fifty years.

I have always loved visiting at the school. Occasionally I've been asked to speak to students, such as eighth grade students who are making an oral history of the school, and also to high school classes. I still love the classroom, and I enjoy these opportunities to keep in touch. Ruth and I started monthly luncheons for retired Kinkaid teachers and staff. There are about forty retirees living in the Houston area. This is another important way to stay in touch with friends from the school.

When I took my formal retirement, there was a wonderful retirement party for me put on by Phyllis Selber and a group of mothers from the school. Sam Windsor, who is the only other surviving teacher hired by Mrs. Kinkaid, took his retirement on the same day. I had been presented with a huge photograph of me to be hung in the middle school hallway. Several days after it was in place, someone cut out the photo but left the frame. The teachers and my son kidded me about how someone either loved me or needed the photo for target practice with darts. I was given a smaller sized version of the same photo, which hangs in the hallway of our home. Eventually the insurance company paid for the stolen photo, and a replacement copy is now in the middle school library.

Former students invariably recall incidents from

the past involving me. Just recently I was reminded of when some unknown middle school students painted a mustache on the painting of one of the most important trustees of the school.

The students reminded me that this made me so angry that I called a special assembly and scolded them as a First Sergeant might. One lady who had been present at the time told me that I was the first adult she had ever seen be that angry. I remember how a group of eighth grade boys got together and told one of the men teachers to inform me that they would take care of the problem.

By the next day the portrait was in good shape. Although the guilty party was never identified, the leader of the boys' group informed us that they had taken care of things, and nothing like that would ever happen again. Nothing like that did ever happen again, until my photo disappeared.

Shortly before my retirement, Ruth found her long lost niece. Ruth's brother Ted and his wife had a child named Bonnie in the early 1960s. There was a divorce, and Bonnie's mother took Bonnie and hid her from her father for many years. Bonnie had a step brother, Mitchell, who worked in Houston. Ruth found his name in the telephone book, called him, arranged to meet him, and reconnect Bonnie and Mitchell with our family. We met with Bonnie, her husband Bobby, and their two boys, Brian and Christopher. We are now very close to this family. I love them very much. They are genuine people.

Our nephew Brian is in college now and plans to become a minister. His younger brother, Christopher, is in high school and enjoys life. He is very thoughtful and like his brother, very fun to be with. Bonnie is a Dental Hygienist, and her husband Bobby works for the local power company in East Texas. He keeps very busy with

Art Goddard

a side job. He is really dedicated to his family.

On my side of the family, all are gone except two second cousins who live in Massachusetts. One of these, Tony Barrett and his wife Janet, are close to us.

They have visited with us and correspond regularly. We look forward to seeing them when they can travel down to Houston. He is a surveyor and she is a nurse.

When Ruth and I moved to the Spring Branch area, we decided to change our church membership from the First Methodist Church to Fair Haven United Methodist Church, which was in the Spring Branch area.

I joined the choir there in 1957 and still sing with that choir. I love Christmas time and Easter. My two favorite songs, "Oh Holy Night" and "The Holy City", are performed at those respected times of the year When my parents moved to Houston in 1958, they too joined Fair Haven Church, and my mother sang in the choir until she was ninety years old.

After my father died, Mother spent a few weeks living with her sister Pearl in Massachusetts. When she received the job as receptionist at Kinkaid School, she decided to live in her own apartment rather close to us. In 1989 I had to place her in a nursing home. She died there in 1991 shortly after her ninety-ninth birthday. She is buried next to my father in Houston's Memorial Oaks Cemetery.

After my retirement, Ruth and I celebrated by going on a cruise to Alaska, and it was most enjoyable. We have dreamed about going again, but I'm afraid it is too late for that.

In 1988 I had cataract surgery on one eye, and the following year on the other. In 1991 I was diagnosed with prostate cancer and since then have taken medication for it rather than surgery. My PSA blood count had dropped to zero and stayed there for ten years. However, as I'm writing, it has risen again, and I now have bone cancer. I just finished radiation, but I'm still on chemotherapy. In 1994 I had colon cancer surgery, which was followed by chemotherapy.

In addition to cancer, I had a major congestive heart failure on New Year's Eve 2001. In spite of all these medical problems, I feel well most of the time and try to be as active as possible. I love life and feel there is so much yet to do. It is hard to grow old, but we all face that.

My mind is sharp, and I test it everyday, either on the piano or by reading books. David likes to give me a hard time when I am exercising my fingers and brain.

When I retired from Kinkaid, Ruth and I decided to build a house on land she had inherited in Cat Spring, Texas. We had no intent to live there, but we wanted a weekend retreat. Today, David is experimenting with fruit trees to see which would grow best on the land. We currently have apricot, apple, persimmon, fig, orange, and some blackberry and grape vines. This is an interesting hobby, but it requires hard work, which David manages. I like wandering thru the trees, seeing if there is fruit. If not, I usually will fuss at David about why not. This keeps us entertained. Now we do not travel on summer vacations; we just spend a few week ends in Cat Spring. We lease about 28 acres of our land for cattle. This gives us an agricultural exemption on taxes for which we are grateful.

Recently we have had more health problems. Ruth was diagnosed as diabetic and is trying hard to deal with it by diet. On Christmas Day 2002, Ruth fell and hurt her back badly. She has a hairline fracture on part of her spine. My prostate cancer returned, and I completed thirty nine treatments of radiation. For nearly six months I seemed to be free of cancer, but one day I popped a rib and a resulting x-ray and bone scan showed I have several bone cancer places. I feel quite well while I write this, but I use a cane when walking outside.

We are very fortunate that our son David enjoys country life. He keeps the Cat Spring property looking nice. He watches the fruit trees, and he hopes to profit from them in the near future–maybe not monetarly, but health-wise.

Before bringing this autobiography to a close, I want to mention how we are all animal lovers. We lease much of the land in Cat Spring to a cattleman. It is interesting to watch the cattle from our front porch there.

We have a German Shepherd thoroughbred named Heidi, and a mixed dog with Australian sheep dog dominate named Sammi. They are our constant companions both in Houston and in the country. I grew up loving animals; these two are no exceptions. I fix for them homemade, fresh healthy treats that they love. The German Shepherd knows how to get what she wants from me. She often rolls her big brown eyes, and who can resist? I know in heaven I will one day see all my animals. They are God's gift to us, and his creation.

My memories are very powerful these days. The Iraqi conflict brought out many "hidden" memories of World War II. I would like to mention that I taught President George W. Bush when he was in the eighth grade. He was a good student of mine. Every teacher would love to say that they taught the President of the United States. That is one reason I have always believed that education is so important. I wrote a note to him congratulating him on his election. I had my heart problem before I could type the note. David found what I had written and arranged thru Don North, headmaster of Kinkaid, for Neil Bush to give it to his brother. Shortly after I returned home from the hospital, I received a call from the White House telling me that the President had received the note and would respond to it personally. I had questioned whether he would remember me.

A few days after the call, I received a note from him stating that not only did he remember me, but that I had made him enjoy reading history. He closed his note by stating, "Now, I'm making history." Little did he know how much history he would be making. September 11, 2001 occurred after that. I pray for him and his leadership of our country.

Chapter 8

Going Home Day

01–23–04

I have found it funny that Dad would go on to his reward on a date that would be a count up–1,23,4. He died just around 6:30pm on the 23rd of January 2004. I do not believe he had any idea his time was near. He was battling cancer and winning, though his heart was taking a beating from the chemo and radiation. His heart was already week from the heart attack he had in Cat Spring on New Year's 2001.

In our last conversation on the 22nd, he was in the hospital. Brought about by the lack of energy, he was very weak. We talked about his need for better eating to regain his strength. I fussed at him for not eating enough and made him eat his breakfast in front of me. As I left, I told him I would see him in the afternoon after work and we were going to make sure he ate well. I would call him during the day to check on him. As I left he said, "Take care of Mom." He had no idea of upcoming events; that was just Dad. I talked to him around lunch time. Mom was there making him eat. He asked when I would be by to see him, I said around 6pm or so. He did seem anxious.

Latter I found out from Mom that she was talking to him on the phone around 4pm and he couldn't talk very well. He told her, "I am not feeling well; I will have to call you back." We never heard him speak again. When I got there around 5pm, he smiled and waved at me, then almost immediately went into a stroke. They had to put him on life support. I spoke to him afterwards, and he understood, but could not reply with all the tubes in him.

I wanted to add a few stories that Dad and I talked about. He was going to include them, but never was able to insert them. They are funny, and for those former students who might have been scared of Dad, this might put a smile on your face.

Dad has a life-long friend who lives in the North East, George Dutton. They grew up together. They, along with George Cragin, once went to New York and saw an incredible amount of shows in one day: movies, Broadway shows and operas. George had reminded me that growing up, Dad had this dog named Bozo. Dad trained Bozo to follow his friends' home and then come back. George said all he had to do was tell him "go home, Bozo."

There was a Washington D.C. trip that Dad, Joe Ludwig and I were on. We had gone up early, as usual. Preparations took time, so Dad always would be up in Washington D.C. before the Chaperones and 8th graders, just to get things organized and to make sure there would be no surprises. We three stayed in a suite. It had three separate rooms and beds, but one doorway to the hall. About 2:30am, we jumped awake to the sounds of

Art Goddard

the hotel fire alarm. All three of us were putting on our cloths and trying to go thru the door into the hallway at the same time. It looked like something out of a comedy. As we were trying to squeeze thru and still put clothes on, the alarm changed to being a false alarm.

Dad was a great cook. Sometimes he loved to experiment, and it would be successful. My work would allow me to come home for lunch. Sometimes I would have to work late, so I wasn't home for supper. While working I would call to check on everybody. Dad would usually ask, "Coming home for lunch?" And in the afternoon he would call: "Will you make it home for supper? We can wait."

Heidi, our German Shepherd, really knew how to communicate with Dad. He loved it.

If she wanted a cookie, she would stare at him from her chair. He would try to ignore her. She would then start making low-level noises. When that would not work, she would put two legs on the floor with the rest of her body still in the chair and get a little louder on her begging. Dad would finally look at her and say, "Well all right." She knew she won.

Once Dad had my cousin's husband Bobby drive him to Cat Spring. I must have been working. It was just the two of them. As Bobby tells the story, during the trip Dad kept looking at a bag of circus peanuts that Bobby had. Bobby asked him if he wanted one. Dad told him he had not had those since he was a boy. Circus peanuts are sweet; they are not peanuts found at a circus. Anyway, before they knew it, they went thru the whole bag. Dad always kept his "child-like" heart.

Dad had commented on how funny life could be. All the years he worked at Kinkaid before he and Mom married, he would go home to be with his parents either at Christmas or in the summer. Taking the train out of Houston, there would be stops at a couple of cities he would later get to know very well. These cities, Sealy and Bellville, are in Austin County, about 11 miles apart from Cat Spring. He would say, "Who would know that some day I would have a place in that area? Mom's family was from that area.

The music ability Dad had always amazed me. People know about his voice, but few knew the full extent of his talent. He would never flaunt it.

He would get on the piano at home and play through music, opera, patriotic tunes, show tunes, and church hymns without any music in front of him. He had this music gift to hear music and apply it without always having to see it.

Dad cared about the importance of education and discipline. Teaching is a gift.

One of Dads former students, Susan Santangelo, who latter became a fellow teacher at Kinkaid and, friend to Dad has a good story to tell. "In 8th grade Mr. Goddard asked our class what careers we might like to train for in College. When I said 'teaching', Mr. Goddard replied 'Be careful that you mean it, for teaching is not a job, it is a calling. Its requirements are very different from those praised in the business world. Its rewards, however, are much greater'"

He loved animals, mostly dogs, he had one cat by the name of Fez who really bonded with him. And he loved his friends, those he kept up with from his early years and those new friends he made all these years living in Houston and he loved his family.

Thank you, Dad, for being who you are and were.

I have to add a thank you to individuals who helped me put the finishing touches on Dad's book. Your help was needed, I am greatly appreciative of your time.

Thank you to: George Dutton, life long friend of Dads. Richard Workman, Ted and John from Dads second breakfast gang, David Veselka, Charles Sanders, Susan Santangelo, John Germann and, Leah Germann.

David Goddard

Grandmother

Christmas 1959 Art and David
(taken by Ruth Goddard)

Christmas
1960
Ruth, Art
and David.
Ruth is
holding
Michelle.

With Grammie

Art and Ruth's Wedding

Art Goddard before WW II

Art Goddard at Kink\aid's
Richmond Campus

Portrait after serving in US Army

Art on right with
Wally "Bunny" Daniels
(Art's cousin) in France WW II

Art on left, WW II

Art's tent
and foxhole
WW II

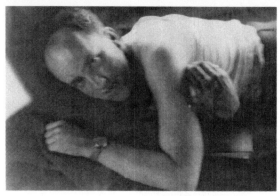

Art Goddard WW II

Bronze Star

LST picture taken by Art

Art on 8th grade
Washington trip
to Gettysburg

Art, Ruth and
David with
Becky in
Cat Spring

Heidi

Art's last 8th grade trip 1989

Art and Ruth on Alaskan Cruise

Ruth and Art Goddard 50th Anniversary

Bonnie Pauler, Ruth, Christopher Pauler, Art, Brian Pauler at high school graduation

Ruth and Art Goddard 40th Anniversary

Sammy

Contact David Goddard
bark@chilitech.com

or order more copies of this book at

TATE PUBLISHING, LLC

127 East Trade Center Terrace
Mustang, OK 73064

888.361.9473

Tate Publishing, LLC

www.tatepublishing.com

CPSIA information can be obtained at www.ICGtesting.com
Printed in the USA
BVOW03s0203300414

352140BV00001B/6/P